LINDROS

DOING WHAT'S
RIGHT FOR

ERIC

LINDROS

DOING WHAT'S
RIGHT FOR

ERIC

Daniel Poulin

Introduction by William Houston

First Edition

Canadian Cataloguing in Publication Data
   Poulin, Daniel, 1944–
     Lindros: doing what's right for Eric

   ISBN 0-9696008-0-1

   1. Lindros, Eric.   2. Nordiques de Québec
(Hockey Team).   I. Title.

GV848.5.L55P684 1992   796.962'092   C92-090217-0

Typesetting/Colour Separations by
  Compeer Typographic Services Ltd.

Printed in Canada by Webcom Limited

To Marie, my only sister

TABLE OF CONTENTS

Acknowledgements

A number of people were very generous with their time and help in preparing this book. In particular my brother Jean-Pierre who acted as my literary agent. Numerous researchers were also helpful namely: Monty Charness, Yves Blouin, Jean-Francois Poirier, Martine Mailly, Ghislaine Pagé, Hélène Tremblay and Jean-Michel Trussart. Finally, many thanks to Jerome Dupont at Panda Publishing Inc., Jim Chalmers at the Canadian Manda Group. Addison Wesley and George Bryson without who's cooperation this book would not have come to fruition.

INTRODUCTION

Is there anyone in Canada—for that matter, is there a hockey fan in the world—who does not have an opinion on Eric Lindros?

In Quebec the widely held perception of Eric is one of a misguided teenager who has arrogantly and selfishly rejected the Quebec Nordiques. Elsewhere, there has been less condemnation. Most people in English Canada, I suspect, side with Eric and accept his reasons for not playing in Quebec.

Why? Some may genuinely believe he has a right to decide where he plays hockey—that the National Hockey League draft, the mechanism that landed Lindros in the hands of the Quebec Nordiques, is fundamentally illegal. If a player has the misfortune of getting drafted by a team that doesn't interest him, he should be accommodated and traded to another. But would there be as much sympathy for Lindros if he had said no to a team in English Canada? The Winnipeg Jets, perhaps, or even the Toronto Maple Leafs?

There are a lot of dynamics at work here. Daniel Poulin notes that the media outside Quebec has been almost uniformly supportive of Lindros, but he makes it clear that sports writers have their own agenda. Some, it would seem, feel it important to become friends of the athletes they cover, especially the stars. If Wayne Gretzky is a "friend," if you can call him "Gretz" and he addresses you by your first name, then it becomes a status symbol. It makes you special.

That's one of the elements of the story—journalists toadying up to young Eric and his family, knowing that in the years to come he will be one of the most important and influential hockey players in the NHL. In the context of the media, Eric's mother and father are portrayed as parents who attempt to influence and even manage the news of their son. On this subject, I can offer one anecdote.

More than a year ago, Bonnie felt that the coverage of Eric in *The Globe and Mail* was overly negative. She wrote a letter of complaint to the editor-in-chief and then, through phone calls, pressed for a meeting to air the family's grievances.

To my knowledge, there had been only one story that could be construed as negative. Neil A. Campbell had reported that Eric, at the age of 17, was already getting paid to attend card shows and sell his autograph. Campbell tried several times to reach Lindros's agent, Rick Curran, but Curran didn't return the calls until after the story appeared.

The Lindros's letter arrived a few months later and was prompted by a note in my column, stating that Eric would never play in Quebec, citing Bill Watters, Curran's former partner, as the source. Team Lindros (mom, dad, family lawyer and Curran) immediately jumped into action. Curran called Watters on the morning the story appeared and expressed, loudly and clearly, his unhappiness. Bill eventually sent the Lindros family a short note, stating that his remarks were strictly his opinion and had been made over the radio. Curran, meanwhile, denounced my report, calling it a fabrication and saying that Quebec was still an option for Eric. We all know what has happened since then.

Anyway, Bonnie and Carl got their meeting with the *Globe's* managing editor and sports editor, and from what I heard it went well. They expressed their concerns, the *Globe* listened and explained its position. Both sides parted amicably.

Since then, I have occasionally poked fun at Bonnie and family in my column. I don't think any of it has been malicious, although I did talk to one NHL general manager who surprised me with his strong concerns about Eric — the fact that he might be difficult to coach and may not get along with his team-mates. "And not only that," added the general manager. "If you get Eric, you get his mother." I used the quotation and it ran with a cartoon of Bonnie, who happens to be an attractive woman, depicted as a bag lady and chasing after her son with a hockey stick in her hand.

But I digress. Daniel Poulin has known the family since Eric was a 16-year-old hockey phenomenon. He has been to their home and talked at length with Bonnie and Carl. He was one of the first television journalists to do a comprehensive feature on Eric.

He was even able to get young Eric to say in French (remember, this was three years ago) that he would be happy to play in Quebec City. "Oui, j'aimerais jouer pour les Nordiques ou les Canadiens; c'est vrai, oui." (Yes, I'd like to play for the Nordiques or the Canadiens, sure.)

A lot has happened since then. In Quebec, Eric's anti-Nordiques position is seen as analogous to the rejection and hostility Quebecers feel from English Canada as a whole. I'm not going to put words into Eric's mouth, but I think it's important to remember that his attitude reflects the feeling of a large number of Canadians and, I would argue, mirrors that of Quebec.

Rejection is felt on both sides. If Quebec is intent on separating, why should Eric want to be part of it? I think that's a fair question. Right or wrong, the Nordiques are paying a price for doing business in a province that has nationalistic aspirations.

From Daniel Poulin, a French-speaking Quebecer who has lived outside the province for 20 years, we get a book with a point of view. It's not an attack on Eric. Instead, it's an attempt to come to grips with the changing attitudes of a high-profile family living in a country bitterly divided between French and English. It's an attempt to understand the Lindroses, and what he finally sees he doesn't like.

You may not agree with Daniel. But you'll read what he has to say. He has given us an insightful and often fascinating look at the most important Canadian sports story of the 1990s.

William Houston

PREFACE

I don't know Eric Lindros. I've never met the man. But what he has come to represent, I have met time and again. A none too subtle example of the misunderstanding and ignorance which fills the gulf between two nations struggling as one. All set against the backdrop of hockey, our national game. One hell of a story.

I wouldn't be in his shoes for all the money . . . for all the money he will probably earn on the rinks of the National Hockey League and more importantly — at least it appears Mr. Lindros thinks so — the megadollars involved in endorsements.

The issue goes far beyond Eric Lindros and the Lindros family. Their reluctance to involve themselves with Les Nordiques and the city of Québec I have to assume stems from ignorance and fear. We fear what we don't understand and therein lies the crux of the matter.

That such ignorance still beats in the bosom of English Canada does not surprise me; but that its pulse pounds such a strong course is indeed frightening. We have seen in the recent past all too many examples of an English backlash against the francophone assertion of rights and beliefs within the framework of this nation. On one level we have a man, a man who says no. No to a city, a language, a culture, and in the end, a nation. More is the pity.

I know Quebec City. I've worked there. Played some hockey there. At least I think I did. Perhaps it was a dream; it often felt like one. The point being there is so much to be gained for this man by playing for Les Nordiques. He sees not the advantages, the challenges and richness that would come from such a reality. Instead, he believes his fears and loses out.

On this side I feel sorry for Eric Lindros. His youth and ignorance are robbing him of the glorious chance to grow. As a player and, what's certainly more important, as a person.

I don't rightly remember when I first met Daniel Poulin. All I know is that it was some years ago. But I'm quite certain this recollection poses no problem for him. The man is, after all, a reporter. I'm sure he could tell me what day it was, the circumstances, even the phase of the moon; such is his sense of "history".

A veritable storehouse of knowledge, from hockey to Horowitz, he is a well-rounded man. And I do mean well rounded. Don't get me wrong. Unlike Tintin reporter, I can't see him chasing two thugs running for the last train out of Zagreb. Daniel Poulin would be more likely to chase Pat Burns for the last donut at a Canadiens press conference.

But there is no denying his worth as a scrupulous and honest newsman in the world of sport. Undoubtedly, not a familiar name in Quebec, Daniel Poulin's reputation in Toronto is one of fairness and thoroughness. One thing about him puzzles me, though. After years of covering the Toronto Maple Leafs, he has retained his sanity. Truly a remarkable feat! . . .

I hope you enjoy this book as much as I have. A fascinating and insightful look at the machinations of the "business" of hockey.

Carl Marotte
Actor and star of the TV series *He Shoots, He Scores*

PRESENTATION

Eric Lindros may well be the most important sports personality I have yet had the opportunity to meet, primarily because his career as a hockey player has developed under such unusual circumstances. From the outset, I felt Lindros was a young man destined for extra-ordinary success on the world sports scene. However, as a result of the controversial position taken by the young athlete, I began to ask myself some serious questions about the underlying motives of the Lindros clan, as they can be called. I then had to look at the possible consequences of the Lindroses' absolute refusal to consider the Quebec option for their exceptionally talented son.

This work of investigative journalism uses a series of interviews with many people who have been associated with Eric Lindros to a greater or lesser degree. The goal of the interviews is twofold: to try and see what is behind the exterior façade presented by the Lindroses, and to shed a little light on the complex negotiations between two parties as far removed from one another as are the two cultural communities of our country.

Above all, the Lindros story clearly illustrates the fact that the members of the press in Quebec and Ontario are deeply divided, having taken opposite sides in this debate. In Quebec, the press has tried to be as objective as possible in analyzing the position taken by Eric and the Lindros clan. In Toronto, however, the press has made no attempt to question the statements made by the clan but has taken everything said at face value. The bulk of the Toronto sports community seems to have given its full support to this player who will surely dominate the national sport of a country that is no longer certain of its own political direction.

As for the hockey establishment, it has been caught in the middle. Its members certainly want to see the Quebec Nordiques succeed in their negotiations with Eric Lindros; but they also do not want to see too much time pass before the young hockey player joins their ranks. By his very presence, this giant of an athlete should help popularize a sport which is in desperate need of new heroes, especially in some parts of the United States where the image projected by hockey is still a negative one.

Ultimately, the Lindros story is the human tragedy of a young man whose education has taught him to be almost exclusively preoccupied with material concerns and pointed him in one direction only. He has learned to be rather narrow-minded and not at all open to the contemporary concept of the world as a global village.

FOREWORD

"NO SPORT HAS CONTROLLED ITS ATHLETES AS EFFORTLESSLY AND TOTALLY AS HOCKEY"[1]

The above assertion describes a view that is gaining universal acceptance among informed observers on the sports scene. David Cruise and Allison Griffiths make this striking statement and back it up in very clear and convincing terms in their excellent book, *Net Worth*, an exploration of the myths of professional hockey. Near the end of the book, the authors make another observation which is worth repeating:

". . . when the NHL does something for *the good of the game* it really means for *the good of the owners*. And he's determined to turn that understanding to his advantage."[2]

"He" is Eric Lindros.

The world of hockey has never had to deal with an individual like Eric before. Not only is he difficult, he is surrounded by his parents, who are as convinced of the rightness of his attitude as he is, and by two able advisors, his agent Rick Curran and his lawyer Gord Kirke. Together, these five people can be referred to as "the Lindros clan".

Q. Tell me honestly, Eric. Who really makes the decisions about your future?

A. I make all my own decisions. We all put our cards on the table and discuss things as a group, but in the end, I'm the one who makes the decisions.

When Eric talks to you, he does so with enormous self-confidence. Unlike other professional athletes, who almost all seem uncomfortable when they have to answer the brilliant or not so brilliant ques-

---

1 Cruise, David and Allison Griffiths. *Net Worth*, p. 5.
2 *Ibid.*, p. 356.

tions of journalists, their eyes darting here and there or staring blankly into space, Eric does not hem and haw. He looks you right in the eye and he gives you straight answers.

His direct approach makes it impossible to doubt his truthfulness when he says that he alone makes the final decisions for the clan. Questions can be raised, however, about how he comes to think what he thinks and to say all that he says, especially in view of the silly, ridiculous statements he occasionally utters in public, which leave something to be desired in terms of their suitability or pertinence.

Q. Did you really say that you would be willing to play in Montreal but not in Quebec City?

A. Yes I did.

Q. Why?

A. I'm not exactly sure. Maybe because Montreal is more of a big city than Quebec, and to me it seems more open, less provincial. It's hard to explain. I just know I would be more comfortable there.

As usual, Eric's answers are frank and honest, but they are sometimes thoughtless and show a striking lack of judgment. Perhaps someone should remind him that some truths are better left unsaid, although such advice would probably fall on deaf ears. A quick look through Eric's autobiography is enough to show that getting your message across to him may not be easy. Indeed, he admits that he was not a model student and that as a youngster he took shortcuts to avoid hard work. Eric's autobiography also indicates that his parents observed early on that their older son liked to do as he pleased.

In that regard, however, he takes after his parents. Carl and Bonnie Lindros are a solidly united couple. Always on the same wave length, they share a desire to see their children succeed and help them in whatever way they can. For example, once they realized how exceptionally talented Eric really was, they immediately established the necessary priorities, even though he was only nine years old. They consulted as many experts as they could find and, at the suggestion of Doug Orr, father of the famous Bobby, they began their association with Rick Curran.

Carl Lindros has said in private how much he has enjoyed watching his son develop under his guidance. He is particularly proud of the self-confidence Eric displays for the media, especially in front of microphones and cameras.

In some instances, Eric's self-confidence makes him appear arrogant and self-important, and to some people, the tone he has adopted in recent months may seem presumptuous. However, those who know him well are quick to point out that he is not really like that.

Most of his teammates on the Oshawa Generals of the Ontario Hockey League will tell you that Eric "does not have an ounce of vanity in him". His coach Rick Cornacchia says that Eric does not like to steal the limelight and that, on the contrary, he always insists on being accompanied by another player when he receives an honour.

Of course, these statements were made last season, in the spring of 1991. It is now many months later and there has been a lot of water under the bridge. In the interval, Eric Lindros has changed in some unusual ways.

Chapter 1

FIRST ENCOUNTER

I first encountered Eric Lindros in the fall of 1989, when he was playing for a Detroit team in an amateur junior tournament. His name was already making the rounds among those in the know in college hockey circles, and several scouts had come to watch him play. People were saying that he would be another Gretzky, perhaps even greater than the Great One. The old arena where the fairly obscure competition was taking place was jam packed, if for no other reason than because so many of the players' parents and friends were there. Despite the obvious partisanship felt by large groups of spectators for the local players, most of the crowd seemed unusually excited. A sense of expectation wafted on the rarified air. People were obviously waiting for the appearance of the player whose name was already on everyone's lips.

As the players came out on the ice, the crowd held its breath for a moment, as if people were waiting to show how pleased they were to see the eagerly awaited sensation skate into view. And he *was* sensational! In the presence of all those wonderfully gifted young athletes Eric Lindros stood out, even before the game began. Standing almost six foot five and weighing more than two hundred pounds, the boy who was not quite sixteen was every inch a man.

All eyes were on him. No one missed a single move or talked of anything else. His presence made itself felt throughout the game, from beginning to end. People were especially aware of how strong he was.

Indeed, more often than not, words of praise are directed at his physical power. True, Lindros can score plenty of goals, and true, he can impress the crowd with the precision of his passes and the beauty and polish with which he executes some of his manoeuvres. But what the experts admire, what really blows them away is that, in addition to his exceptional talents as a playmaker, he seems to have the need to crush his opponents, to beat them into the ground so that afterwards he can better control the game. His impressive physical prowess has helped him to master every aspect of the game as no one before him has ever done.

"Amazing" is the word most scouts use when they talk about Eric, even though, having seen many talented players over the years, they are not so easily carried away by what other people too often tend to describe as out of the ordinary.

Eric Lindros *is* out of the ordinary, on several accounts. It is easy to say of him that he is head and shoulders above his peers—that much, after all, is obvious. What differentiates him from other hockey players of his generation is his mind. In his early days of junior hockey, when he was only sixteen and playing with Americans who were all older but less talented than he, the pertinent, spontaneous way he thought out his game, devoid of the usual clichés so common in the world of sports, was already setting him apart from his fellow players.

I had telephoned Eric's father before going to the game. We had a brief conversation, during which we arranged to meet in the evening to do an interview for a story to be shown at a later time on *La Soirée du Hockey*, Radio-Canada's equivalent of *Hockey Night in Canada*. That first conversation with Carl Lindros left me with a very positive impression. Warm, friendly and courteous, he seemed to be a man who was both pleasant and approachable. We had another conversation later, when we met at the game between periods, and that too went well. Carl Lindros appeared receptive to the idea of doing a portrait of Eric for French-language television and even invited us to shoot it at the Lindros home. We couldn't say no to a proposition like that.

Needless to say, we were feeling pretty enthusiastic as we made our way to the Lindros home that evening. When I say we, I mean Pierre Gendron, the cameraman, Jean-François Poirier, a young journalism student who was new in Toronto and spoke hardly any English, and me with a Radio-Canada microphone in my hand. The house is in an affluent, upper middle class Toronto neighbourhood, where properties are known to be worth more than half a million dollars each. It may not be the richest area in the city, but the residents are certainly well off.

When you first walk into the Lindros home you are immediately struck by its spotless appearance and the simplicity of the furnishings. The ground floor has a medium sized living room and a modern, functional kitchen, which looks like a pleasant room to be in. Upstairs are the bedrooms, one of which Eric shares with his younger brother

B__ was there that we began our work by having a nice friendly chat with Brett who, to my great surprise, managed to converse quite well in French. Brett made no secret of his admiration for his big brother. He sang Eric's praises, going on in that enthusiastic way which is so characteristic of healthy, high-spirited boys his age. One of our exchanges went as follows:

Q. What is it that fascinates you most about your brother?
R. That's easy. His strength and the way he likes to fight.

That assessment is shared in one way or another by several observers, who see in Eric a tendency towards tough, aggressive play. Some commentators use the word "physical" to describe Eric's style.

Our conversation with Brett lasted about twenty minutes and served to set the stage for the ultimate purpose of the story — the interview with Eric. Once we had finished shooting Brett's part, he offered to go and find his brother, to warn him that it was now his turn to take the hot seat.

A few minutes later, Eric appeared at the top of the stairs and greeted the three of us very politely, shaking hands with each of us in turn. Our first encounter was quite positive, with virtually nothing to suggest a clash of wills. The atmosphere was lighthearted — the bedroom that Eric and Brett shared was decorated in a style popular among modern teenagers, and it provided an excuse to engage in some harmless, good-natured kidding.

The decor also threw a little light on the boys' views and attitudes. Not surprisingly, one corner of the room was filled with Eric's trophies, although by that stage of his development they represented only minor achievements and seemed to hold little interest for him. What really engaged the boys' attention was the parade of pin-ups displayed on both sides of the room, as if each wanted to prove he had better taste than the other, and that someday one of these women would probably be part of another collection, a trophy won in the chase.

Normally, when young athletes have to do a television interview, they exhibit signs of tension and insecurity, quite natural in young people confronted by a stranger asking questions likely to annoy or

4

provoke even the brightest among them. If Eric Lindros harboured any such feelings, he did a good job of hiding the fact. He didn't even ask the question we expected, the one we usually hear in such circumstances — What are you going to ask me? On the contrary, he suggested that we go right ahead with the interview, without reservations and without any rehearsal.

Q. Are you aware that you've already made a name for yourself?

R. Sure, I read the papers and watch TV like everybody else.

Q. What effect does it have on you?

A. It doesn't bother me at all. In fact, I think it's funny. Anyway, there's nothing I can do about it.

Q. Are there any subjects you would rather not talk about in the interview?

A. I don't like being asked questions unrelated to hockey.

The questions were brief and unprovocative — one cliché after another — and Eric followed suit with short, conventional answers. The interview went on this way until the end. At that point I asked Eric if he would be willing to answer, in French, a simple question about the possibility of his playing professional hockey in Quebec one day. We literally put the words in his mouth, with an assist from Brett who suddenly felt appreciated in relation to his big brother. After Eric had practised the sentence about a dozen times and I could see he was pronouncing it as well as he could, I decided to go ahead and record the sequence. I asked him if he would like to wear a Quebec Nordiques or Montreal Canadiens sweater one day.

He answered "Oui; j'aimerais jouer pour les Nordiques ou les Canadiens; c'est vrai, oui". (Yes, I'd like to play for the Nordiques or the Canadiens. Sure.)

To end the conversation I jokingly called out in English "Liar!", to which he replied "I know! . . .". The whole exchange was followed by a very telegenic burst of laughter.

I did not realize how charming that short sequence was until it was being edited. The editor suggested that to make Eric look better we should cut out the teasing, which was amusing but unnecessary in a public broadcast, and end the story with the shot of him laughing.

At the time, no one could predict how events would unfold, even though the Quebec Nordiques seemed to be heading into another losing season. After all, Eric would not be available for the draft coming up that season, and it was always possible that the Nordiques would improve sufficiently before the name of Lindros rose to prominence in 1991. Therefore, Eric was not worried about tossing out a statement which would be heard by *La Soirée du Hockey* audiences one Saturday evening in winter, and in French to boot, saying that he would like to play for the Nordiques.

It would be interesting to have Eric listen to that extract today, and even more interesting to see what reaction those words would trigger in his parents.

No doubt, the laugh would disappear from Eric's face or, if not, he would probably turn pale . . .

During the famous press conference at Le Colisée de Québec on the night of the Team Canada game against the U.S.S.R., as it was then known, a reporter asked Eric, "Is it true that you said on television, in French, that you would like to play for the Quebec Nordiques someday?"

In reply, Eric said, "I don't think so, because I couldn't have said that much in French."

That day, Eric certainly proved that he had an amazing ability to handle himself in embarrassing situations, knowing full well that in the given circumstances, it would not have been easy for him to say anything without irritating his audience, to say the least.

After we had finished talking with Eric we went downstairs, where we waited for his parents. Carl kindly did a short interview with us in the living room. A large, impressive-looking man with piercing eyes, and quite talkative and friendly, Carl was willing to speak to us about anything that concerned his son, remembering to make frequent references throughout the interview to the other family members. You sensed that he wanted to project an image of a close-knit family. He even managed to mention the name of Eric's little sister Robin, not for any particular reason, merely to let us know that she existed and had a place in the story. He also alluded here and there to Eric's mother Bonnie, who always plays a role in the decision-making process.

Since neither of Eric's parents speak French, I decided to keep the interview with Carl short, and I suggested to Gendron that he use his imagination to shoot a family scene in the kitchen with, if possible, Eric and his mother. Gendron is a talented, skilful and very meticulous cameraman. While he was working at getting his lighting right, I spent the time talking a bit with Bonnie while she was preparing a snack for Eric and a friend of his, who is also a hockey player, and whose father was a well-known referee in the National Hockey League. Everything was quite natural, as if we weren't there, and Bonnie was kind enough to do what the cameraman asked of her. The scene finally looked good enough for it to be included in the story. It consisted of Bonnie asking Eric a question and Eric giving a short answer, and it was used to provide a link between two statements by the hero. All told, the story took only three minutes, in accordance with the formula regarding cut-ins on *La Soirée du Hockey*.

This would be the Lindroses' first appearance on the French network of Radio-Canada. A brief portrait, of course, but a rather pleasant picture of a typical family unit.

Everything seemed to have gone well, and it looked as if we were off to a good start all around. We were smiling when we left at the end of the evening, already wondering when our paths would cross again and in what circumstances.

A few weeks later, the name Lindros was appearing in the headlines with increasing frequency, in particular because the Ontario Hockey League had finally given in to the demands of the Lindros clan and changed the rules to accommodate Eric.

The Sault Ste. Marie Greyhounds had acquired the rights to the young superstar in the midget draft, even though Eric's parents had informed the league that their son would report only to a team based in southern Ontario, with Oshawa as first choice since it was closest to Toronto.

One of the league rules stipulated that a player picked in the first round of the midget draft could not be traded during his first season in the league. Therefore, it looked like Lindros would have to wait until the following year before he could demonstrate his talents at that highly competitive level. An exception could be made, however, if the impact of the player was considered important enough to the league. Such was the case with Eric. The Board of Governors of the league quickly decided to revise both its position and its rule and to allow the Greyhounds to make a deal. As Bonnie and Carl Lindros had wished, the Oshawa Generals acquired young Eric and, in return, the Greyhounds obtained three players, two draft choices and the sum of $80,000. The very day after the deal was made, large numbers of fans appeared at Oshawa's Civic Auditorium to buy whatever tickets were still available for the Generals' remaining home games that season. Eric's arrival had moved the Oshawa team, already considered one of the best in the league, another step closer to being the season champions. They were crowned the following spring. The Generals not only won the league championship, they captured the Memorial Cup as well, making them Canadian Junior Champions. At 17, Eric Lindros had clearly demonstrated what the experts had predicted — his presence on a team could take it to the top.

Not everyone agreed with the decision of the league's Board of Governors. Orval Tessier, who was general manager of the Cornwall Royals at the time, readily says that he was against the rule change.

Q. Were you the only one to object?

A. No. Three or four of us general managers were totally against such a proposition.

Q. But didn't you have to have the unanimous consent of the league managers to make such a major change?

A. The final decision rested with the owners. They were quick to see their advantage.

Obviously, the rink is not the only place where Eric makes an impact.

A little earlier, Lindros had played well at a different and even more prestigious level, in the World Junior Hockey Championship in Finland in 1990. As a member of the Canadian team, which won the tournament that year, he had the opportunity to demonstrate his talents. Being on the team can be a very emotional and enormously demanding experience in every way, especially when the tournament is far from home, as it was that year.

Furthermore, the decision to invite Lindros to participate in the tournament was far from unanimous, given his inexperience in major junior hockey. Guy Charron, head coach of the talented team, stated at the time that the decision to include Lindros had not been taken lightly. Eric arrived at training camp in top condition, and his attitude impressed Charron, who had found him a little too individualistic the previous summer. Charron recounts that he came to Eric's room one night to chat. When Lindros asked what was expected of him, Charron turned the question back to him:

Q. What do you expect your contribution to be?

A. I just want to fit into any role where you feel I can help and the only thing that matters is what the team does. I just want to do what the coaches think is best for me.

And he did that — admirably. Everyone agreed that the Canadian victory was really a team victory, with no one player stealing the limelight.

Mike Ricci, one of the better players who formed part of the team, knew Lindros quite well, first as a rival and then as a team-mate, and he cannot praise Eric enough. Ricci was considered the best prospect of 1990 by a number of analysts and came within a hair's breadth of playing for the Quebec Nordiques that year. Today he plays for the Philadelphia Flyers, a team Eric's parents would allow their son to play for.

Q. Is Lindros as good as all that?

A. He's not only an excellent player who's going to get better, he's a very mature guy. He has strong discipline and nothing gets in the way of hockey. That's number one with him and that's how it must be.

It is not uncommon to hear adults pay such homage to young hockey players, but when a player as talented as Ricci does it, and in such articulate terms, we ought to pay some attention.

No doubt about it, Eric Lindros is in a class by himself. He is not only a gifted athlete but also a person with extraordinary qualities. Ultimately, it is these qualities that set him apart from most of the other young athletes of his generation.

When people say that Lindros is an impact player, they are not exaggerating in the least. He makes an impact on almost everyone around him, from the players and managers of a team to the big bosses of an organization. In fact, the entire public is generally swept off its feet by his charm and charisma.

Without question, Eric Lindros will have a significant influence on future generations.

Chapter 2

OSHAWA: HAPPY DAYS

After winning the ultimate trophy in junior hockey, the Oshawa Generals, led by Eric Lindros, began the 1990-91 season full speed ahead. They were established by all observers as strong favourites to repeat their feat of the previous spring, especially since Lindros had proven beyond any doubt that he had what it took to develop into a top-notch player. In only half a season with Oshawa, Eric had won over those around him, and his natural leadership was doing wonders for his team-mates. That was the opinion of his coach, Rick Cornacchia, who is quite open in saying that he is a Lindros fan. You only have to speak to him for a few minutes to discover that he and Number 88 have a lot in common.

There was, however, a period when things were not so amicable between the Lindroses and the coaches. And I do mean the Lindroses, since Bonnie and Carl have been in the unfortunate habit of meddling in Eric's affairs for a long time. In minor hockey organizations, it is quite common to meet parents who interfere a little too much; usually however, with a little diplomacy, everyone manages to come to an agreement and gradually calm the troubled waters. In the Lindroses' case, it appears that it may not be so easy to reach a compromise.

Furthermore, Bonnie and Carl are the first to admit that not all coaches have been responsive to their aspirations for Eric from the time he took his first steps in peewee hockey. In his autobiography, Eric refers to one coach in particular with whom he did not get along. The coach in question, was Peter Miller,[3] a secondary school teacher.

At first, Miller and the Lindroses got along very well, and Miller was often a guest in the Lindros home. The situation became acrimonious when Eric, because of his immense talent, began to take part in higher calibre tournaments. While he was still playing peewee hockey, he was invited to strengthen the rosters of some bantam teams; this meant a shift in priorities, a change which unfortunately did not please those most directly affected, namely the Marlboro Peewee

---

3   Miller was invited to the University of Wisconsin by Bob Johnson, recently deceased head coach of the NHL Pittsburgh Penguins, to give a talk to more than 250 coaches on all aspects of hockey. More than 150 young people who have played under Miller have already received academic scholarships in the United States.

team. In order to rectify the situation, Paul Lewicki, Miller's assistant, took it upon himself to make it clear to the Lindroses that their first obligation was to the Marlboros as they had agreed earlier. The Lindroses did not at all appreciate being told what to do and from then on, they avoided contact with the other parents, and kept to themselves.

As for Eric, he ate, slept and breathed hockey, to the point where he sometimes managed to play in three or four games on the same day. His coaches could only marvel at his phenomenal performance, which showed an exceptionally high potential energy level that astounded everyone, including Peter Miller.

Q. What was your impression of Eric at that time?

A. Eric had the greatest work ethic. He would practise at two o'clock in the morning if he had to. He always wanted to be the best he could be. He would do his drills at such high intensity that he would hyperventilate and lose his breath. No, there really wasn't anything negative to say about him.

We have to remember that Eric was only twelve years old at the time, and people were already saying that he was way ahead of his team-mates. Not that he was perfect. Far from it, as Paul Lewicki will tell you.

Q. Are you saying Eric wasn't popular?

A. Just that he had no friends on the team.

Q. But what did he do to alienate his team-mates?

A. He would do all sorts of aggravating things, like shoot the puck at other players. Once he even tripped a coach intentionally.

Lewicki likes to compare Eric Lindros to Carl Lewis, the well-known American sprinter, Ben Johnson's eternal rival.

Q. What similarities do you see between Lindros and Carl Lewis?

A. Both are tremendous athletes but both are unliked.

While it may be true that twelve-year-olds can sometimes be cruel, they usually forget quickly and virtually no one holds a grudge at that age. If Eric Lindros had very few friends when he was twelve, it was partly because of his parents. According to his coaches at the time, Bonnie and Carl seemed to have a tendency to alienate people, as illustrated by this story that Paul Lewicki likes to tell. The day the Marlboro Peewees lost the championship, Bonnie Lindros was beaming with joy in spite of the defeat, as she proudly walked around showing off a brand new Young Nationals sweater — the team Eric would be playing for next. It is easy to imagine how uncomfortable she was making her young son whose team had just been eliminated. He was certainly in no mood to laugh, much less to seem petty . . .

Q. Tell me, Mr. Lewicki, how would you describe the Lindroses?

A. The Lindroses are only semi-happy when they call most of the shots.

Lewicki concedes that he himself is no angel. He tells of the day when he learned that Eric was leaving the Marlboros to go to the Young Nats. He spent the evening getting good and drunk, ending up at the Lindros home, where he admits that he put up posters saying, "Go Marlies Go".

Peter Miller is a typical example of a truly dedicated coach; he devotes more than twenty hours a week to working with young hockey players on a volunteer basis. And his credentials are impressive. Besides having a reputation as a highly competent coach, he is athletic director at Henry Carr High School, the most prestigious Catholic secondary school in Toronto. Miller and his wife Carla are among those who have been victims of the Lindroses' abuse to the point where they have had to take extreme measures to put an end to the problem.

Q. How did they show their animosity?

A. Carla, my wife, was accosted one day by Bonnie Lindros who berated her for some hate literature they had apparently gotten.

Q. What did you do?

A. I was forced to send Bonnie a letter on the school letterhead to tell her to stop abusing my wife.

Q. Did that do the trick?

A. Yes. Bonnie never bothered us again.

Miller and Lewicki report that at times the Lindroses have created their own problems. An example of this occurred on the night of the Esso Cup, a competition that brings together the sixteen best peewee hockey teams in Metropolitan Toronto. When it was time for the presentation of the trophy to the Most Valuable Player of the competition, Eric's parents suggested that he go up to get his prize. The presenter saw Eric and asked what the youngster was doing there. When Eric replied that he had come to get his trophy, he was told that he was not the winner. The winner on that occasion was a player named Paul Evans.

The story is that Eric turned around and walked to the back of the arena, looking very disappointed. Without saying a word, he supposedly broke a window with his hockey stick, then left and went out to the parking lot to cry.

Eric Lindros's move from the Marlboros to the Young Nats led to a distinct improvement in the Lindroses' relationship with their son's coach. Ed Robicheau is known for his effectiveness with the young players he instructs. The team he was coaching when Eric arrived already had a number of assets, especially with regard to physical strength, and Eric quickly adapted to the system, since it was so well-suited to his style of play. It may well have been Robicheau who contributed the most to Eric's development—which would certainly explain why he never had any problems with the Lindroses.

Q. What was your first impression of Eric?
A. When Eric was with me, he was playing as an underage. So it would be unfair to say he was the best player on the team. He certainly wasn't the best player when he got here, but as the year progressed, he became the best.
Q. Were you on good terms with his parents?
A. I never had any problems with the Lindroses. They never came up to me and said, "You're not doing this, you're not doing that".

In his autobiography, Eric praises Robicheau highly.

Without taking anything away from Eric's father, Robicheau will tell you that Carl Lindros did not show Eric how to play hockey.

Q. What do you mean by that?

A. His dad didn't teach him the game. He taught him skills.

Q. Then who contributed the most to Eric's development?

A. Eric himself! He was always asking questions. Things that other players just wouldn't ask about the game, he would ask. He was always thinking of questions to ask.

Robicheau's comments are supported by Terry Weir, general manager of the Young Nats. Weir knew Eric's parents very well and had a good relationship with them.

Q. Was it easy to satisfy their demands?

A. In general, yes. Though they were very outspoken, they did everything they could for him. And they were highly supportive.

This tendency to be outspoken sometimes seems excessive and even offensive. It has often placed Eric in embarrassing situations, to the point where he chooses to mention in his autobiography that his mother is very outspoken and that she says what's on her mind. He also adds that she has been known to go a little too far once in awhile. He admits that he discovered early on that his mother was not one to hold her tongue.

The Lindroses had not been living in Toronto long, before people knew who they were, both because Eric made his mark in hockey so quickly and also because Bonnie tended to take a stand on most things.

Nathan Lafayette, of the Cornwall Royals in the Ontario Hockey League played atom hockey with Eric at that time.

Q. What do you recall from that experience?

A. Eric was always the team's leading scorer even though he was younger. It would seem like he would just decide to score and then he'd deke out the whole team and score.

Q. How did the other players feel about that?

A. There was almost no resentment from anyone. But Bonnie, his mother, liked to have her views known. She would think nothing of going down and talking to the coach.

Q. Did it bother you?

A. It didn't bother any of the players, but it bothered the other parents.

Bonnie Lindros herself admits that she talks a lot. And she justifies her behaviour in public by saying that mothers always get upset at the rink when things aren't right.

Another team-mate who knew Eric well is Matt McGuffin. Like Nathan, he too is with the Cornwall Royals today. Matt lived in the same neighbourhood as the Lindroses when he was growing up.

Q. What were his parents like?

A. His father used to come to practices and he showed me some things about crossovers and skating.

Q. And his mother?

A. The whole neighbourhood used to talk about the way his mother was always bragging about her son.

McGuffin adds that Eric Lindros intimidates him now.

Q. Why?

A. Because he is so well known.

Q. Do you resent him?

A. In order to resent him, you have to at least be at his level, and no one in our league is.

The Ontario Hockey League is where most young Ontario players dream of playing when they grow up, hoping they will one day make it to the big time, the National Hockey League. Eric Lindros was no exception to this rule, even if he did have to resort to a little blackmail to achieve his ends. What he does not know, however, since few people do, is that he came within a hair's breadth of playing his junior hockey in Toronto.

The hockey world was shaken in 1988 by an event which few observers believed possible and which can easily be described as the trade of the century. Wayne Gretzky went from the Edmonton Oilers to the Los Angeles Kings. The transaction was due to the appearance on the hockey scene of Bruce McNall, an ambitious, very wealthy man, whose fortune had come partly from numismatics. He is a man who likes to take risks and is used to putting his money on thoroughbreds. McNall, a recent convert to hockey, always has a smile on his face and he is friendly and disarmingly straightforward and unaffected; furthermore, despite his prominence, he has remained relatively accessible. When he first came to Toronto with his Kings dressed for success in their new uniforms, I managed to take McNall aside to make a business proposition I thought might interest him. It involved several names from the world of hockey, of course, each one as distinguished as the next—first McNall, then Harold Ballard, Wayne Gretzky indirectly, and finally Eric Lindros, who was not yet a household name, but soon would be.

To arouse McNall's curiosity, I suggested that he might be able to make an investment that would outwit Harold Ballard without Ballard's being aware of it. Ballard had announced earlier that he had reluctantly decided to put an end to the Toronto Marlboros of the Ontario Hockey League. The Marlies' popularity had been decreasing for several years and the team was playing for smaller and smaller crowds in Maple Leaf Gardens. Even though Ballard told anyone who would listen that the Marlies were dearer to him than the Leafs, he had no choice but to admit that junior hockey was doomed to certain death in Toronto, as in all the other big cities in Canada. But the arrival of Eric Lindros might mean the difference between success and failure for a junior team in a big city—if you could believe the laudatory reports of the scouts who had been following Lindros's development for the last few years.

I therefore proposed that McNall acquire an Ontario Hockey League franchise, stressing the factors that would help make the endeavour a success. He would have the greater Toronto market, which was eager for a winning hockey team; a new logo in the Kings' colours, which had become very fashionable in the hockey world; the involvement of Gretzky, who was extremely popular in Ontario; and finally, the guarantee that Lindros, the new sensation, would be a member of the team.

McNall is a well-informed entrepreneur, and he reacted favourably to my proposal, suggesting that I do some further research and get back to him soon. Without losing any time, I asked for a meeting with Ontario Hockey League president, Dave Branch, who saw me two days later. After Branch had listened seriously to my idea, he said he thought the possibility of a new major junior hockey team in Toronto was very interesting. He assured me that the League governors could be persuaded to vote in favour of the project, and he added that the new team would get the first pick in the next midget draft. That pick would obviously be Eric Lindros. Branch was aware of the value of the future star and he was happy to consider an agreement that would involve McNall, Gretzky and Lindros.

Armed with this favourable reaction, and with the appropriate papers in my pocket, I went to Los Angeles to try to convince McNall to go ahead with the project. Meanwhile, I suggested the idea to some Kings players, including Luc Robitaille, Steve Duchesne and Ron Duguay. All three appeared interested and even enthusiastic, and said they were prepared to invest a little money in such a team which was sure to be successful in the short term — on condition of course, that McNall became the principal shareholder.

Unfortunately, McNall withdrew at the last minute, despite the fact that the project meant an investment of only half a million dollars at that time. The reason put forward by the Kings' owner, however, was quite sound. Wayne Gretzky had apparently advised McNall against going ahead because he did not believe that junior hockey would survive financially. His argument was in all likelihood based on his experience with the Belleville Bulls in the Ontario Hockey League a few years earlier and with the Hull Olympics, in the Quebec Major Junior Hockey League, a team he is still involved with.[4]

If Wayne Gretzky and Bruce McNall had believed in Lindros's potential in 1988, the course of history might have been very different, at least in Ontario because the Sault Ste. Marie incident would never have occurred. There might have been other consequences as well.

---

4 It is interesting to note that Gretzky is at present negotiating with Dave Branch with a view to bringing junior hockey back to Toronto. He is head of a group of investors including John Candy in particular. For the project to succeed, he may have to withdraw from the Hull Olympics in the Quebec Major Junior Hockey League. The arrival of hockey in Ottawa via the National Hockey League, was apparently responsible for Gretzky's change of perspective. The Hull Olympics are already having difficulty surviving, drawing fewer than two thousand spectators per game on average. It would also be a surprise if the Ottawa 67s (OHL) survive.

The Maple Leafs might never have gone ahead with the most bizarre trade in team history, even stranger than the Russ Courtnal–John Kordic transaction. The trade in question saw the arrival of Tom Kurvers in Toronto and forced the Leafs to give up their first round pick in the famous 1991 draft in Buffalo. It is possible to believe that the Nordiques might not have finished last in 1990 if the Leafs had not made a number of transactions, specifically with the Quebec Nordiques, in a desperate attempt to save face. If the Leafs had finished dead last without being able to claim the most coveted young prospect in history since Mario Lemieux, they would have been the laughing stock of just about everyone.

As for the Lindroses, they would certainly have appreciated such an association, since it would have met the criteria they themselves had set with regard to their son's career plan. And it is also possible to believe that the involvement of Robitaille, Duchesne, Duguay and myself, might eventually have led them to change their perception of Francophones — although in light of the stand Eric has taken recently, this is probably doubtful.

As it turned out, it was in Oshawa that Eric would prove himself in 1990 and 1991. The Generals rapidly benefitted from Eric's arrival in 1990, winning fourteen of the nineteen games they played after his insertion in the line-up. And the elimination series enabled Lindros to lead his team to a series of sparkling victories, crowned by their winning the Memorial Cup for the first time in 46 years.

Oshawa rapidly benefitted financially from Eric's presence on the roster as well. In only half a season, the team was able to add more than $100,000 to its coffers. The Generals' success with Lindros on their team cannot help but remind us of the Kings' success with Gretzky in Los Angeles. And just as the National Hockey League profits from the presence of its heros, the Ontario Hockey League is also quick to capitalize on the publicity a player of Lindros's calibre can generate. The Generals are the number one attraction all over Ontario, as well as in Detroit where the Compuware Ambassadors play for the OHL.

Dave Branch smiles with delight when he is asked to talk about Eric Lindros. It is easy to understand why, since he is the one who managed to appease the critics throughout the province when the league allowed the Lindroses to win their case in their initial claim.

Q. Eric must mean a lot to your league?

A. Without question, Daniel. First of all, there's the obvious benefits in terms of the awareness that he's brought to the junior hockey industry. It's not the case that he's just touched the Ontario Hockey League, he's touched junior hockey right across the country, and, I would suggest, in many parts of the United States and Europe. That's the type of impact that he's had.

Branch quickly got to know Eric and he does not hesitate to describe him as an exceptional person in more ways than one. According to Branch, his high opinion of Eric is shared by most of the people who have known Eric in the Ontario Hockey League.

Q. What qualities do you see in him?

A. He is very self-assured, extremely bright, very well organized and very sensitive. He has strong ties with his family and he's not afraid to show his love for his mother. We're very fortunate that the next impact player will be a person that, as a parent, you would be proud to say that your son or daughter idolizes.

Q. You know that not everybody agrees with you?

A. I know there's a bit of a perception out there that he's cold, calculating and totally, you know, let's get on with the business side of the game. I think that, unfortunately, he's had to react like that in some instances because there are so many people out there trying to grab a piece of the action for their own self-gain or their own self-interest.

When Dave Branch is asked to talk about the problem with Sault Ste. Marie, he does so willingly, and even goes so far as to say that the rule change made by the league to accommodate Eric Lindros is one that needed to be made and is a clear improvement on the situation that existed before.

Q. Then why did you wait for the Lindros case to do something?

A. As a league, we were upset at the time because he had actually rebuffed us. Not only did he reject Sault Ste. Marie, but he rejected us as a league. After the emotional factors had settled in, we sat down as a league and said, "This young man is truly exceptional. He's brought something into focus — the ability to trade a first round draft pick". And we went to the family and said, "We're prepared to look at altering our rules to facilitate Eric's playing in our league. Does Eric still want to play in our league?" The answer was yes, and that was basically the end of the discussion. From there we moved forward and made the necessary adjustment which we felt was in the best interest in the short term and also in the long term. And it would also hopefully help teams recruit players by saying, "Hey, if you don't like it or don't think you're going to like it, try it, and then if you still don't like it, we can transfer your playing rights". Before that, we couldn't do that. That led to Rule Number 88.

Q. Isn't it true that you would change your rules again this year, just to accommodate Eric, if you thought you needed to?

A. Not at all. I feel that if we were just to create a loophole for Eric, for one situation only, it would never be adopted by our league. We've got to look at the fact that we've been in business for some fifty years and we hope to be in business for another fifty years. If you just go around creating exceptions, you're not going to last very long.

Dave Branch is not a man to lose his temper easily. As president of the League, he has frequently been called upon to settle stormy arguments; he has also been in the middle of sensitive conflicts between players and coaches or managers. He has always managed to keep his cool. But when he is told that a number of observers think Lindros is being given preferential treatment, he reacts strongly.

Q. What do you say to people who claim that you are at the mercy of the Lindroses?

A. That it's just not true. I know that Eric has always stated to us that he does not want to be treated differently. He's very sensitive as to his peers' perception of him, and in particular his teammates. He's asked on occasion, when we've tried to get involved in different things, to have everyone share in the honours, meaning his team-mates.

It is clear that, except in Sault Ste. Marie where his name is taboo, Eric Lindros enjoys a reputation unequalled in the Ontario Hockey

League, particularly in Oshawa, a city that has always supported its junior hockey team over the years, especially since the time of Bobby Orr, the first real hero to have come from the ranks of the Generals. Thanks to Lindros, moreover, people now speak highly of Oshawa, an unusual experience for that city whose name is more often associated with economic problems, because its economy is subject to the fluctuations of the auto industry. Even the name of the team is derived from the presence of General Motors, the company on which the city depends for its very existence. Politically, Oshawa is an NDP stronghold; former federal NDP leader, Ed Broadbent, was its Member of Parliament for several decades. Since Broadbent was always in the opposition, Oshawa almost never benefitted from government patronage. As a result, journalists tend to disregard this part of Southern Ontario in their daily coverage.

However, Lindros's accomplishments have helped to project a more positive image of the city. And what accomplishments! In his first complete season with the Generals, he was awarded a number of honours. He won the Eddie Powers Memorial Trophy given to the top goal scorer in the league (Eric had 149 points, with 71 goals and 78 assists in only 57 games), and the Red Tilson Trophy for most valuable player in the Ontario Hockey League. Nationally he earned one of the rewards most coveted by junior hockey players in Canada, the Transamerica Life Plus-Minus Award; according to many experts, the plus-minus figure best represents the positive contribution of a player to his team. Lindros finished the season with a plus-74. Eric also received The Valvoline Top Draft Prospect Award, a trophy which, as its name indicates, goes to the player most likely to be selected in the first round of the universal draft.

And there have been other honours. In the Ontario-Quebec junior all-star game, Lindros was named the game's Most Valuable Player for the Ontario team, while Yanic Perreault received the same honour for the Quebec team. The Ontario team was defeated 11 to 7 at the hands of their Quebec counterparts in that exciting game played in the Montreal Forum. And internationally, Eric's star shone even more brightly when he was chosen his team's most valuable forward at the end of the World Junior Hockey Championship, which Canada won.

The Most Valuable Player of the 1990-91 year in Canadian junior hockey was Eric Lindros, and it was pure chance that the trophy, the Molson-Cooper, happened to be awarded in Quebec City during the Memorial Cup Tournament. The recipient is always chosen from among three candidates, one from Ontario, one from Western Canada and one from Quebec. It is amusing to note that the Quebec candidate, Yanic Perreault, was claimed by the Toronto Maple Leafs in the same draft that saw the Quebec Nordiques choose Lindros. As far as I know, Perreault is not complaining about his fate at all.

That Eric Lindros is highly praised in many circles goes without saying; it is also true that he comes in for quite a bit of criticism, and that some of it has reached the ears of the Lindros clan. Rick Cornacchia, the head coach of the Generals, is quick to come to the defense of his protégé whenever he can.

Q. What do you say to his detractors?
A. A lot of people don't know the real Eric Lindros. Once they get to know him, they find he has an excellent character. It's very easy for someone to knock him. The media are always looking for a kink in his armour. Nobody can take away the fact that he is an excellent individual.

When the season began in September 1990, everyone expected Lindros to be at the centre of events in the hockey world in Canada. Increasingly, the headlines were highlighting his accomplishments, and everyone was absolutely sure that he was going to become number one in professional hockey. "The Next One" was the nickname most often used by the press to describe him, a play on Gretzky's richly deserved nickname "The Great One". But some people feel it is a little too early for Lindros to assume this particular mantle.

Since I was aware of the impact Eric would have in the months to come and alert to the possibility that the Quebec Nordiques would again have the first pick in the 1991 draft, I took the initiative and approached Carl Lindros, to make him an offer which I thought at the time, might interest him.

We met at noon one Monday in the fall, at the end of a long weekend. Toronto seemed to be particularly quiet that day and the restaurant we went to at Carl's suggestion was almost deserted. We were therefore able to talk freely without being overheard.

Carl Lindros always impressed me as an open man, willing to listen to other people's ideas, and interested in any suggestions that might contribute to the advancement of his son's career. It therefore seemed perfectly natural for me to make him the following offer:

Q. Carl, would you like to have a documentary video produced, covering Eric's season in Oshawa, showing him working towards the big day, the draft in Buffalo?

A. What do you mean by a documentary video?

The fact that he answered my question with another question did not make me unhappy since it showed that he was not just curious but even somewhat interested. He was also giving me an opportunity to be more specific about my idea. What I was offering the Lindroses in short, was to have a camera follow Eric during his first complete season with the Generals, showing him in real-life situations and capturing some of his reactions as well as his performances. Comments from those around him would be added, and the tape would conclude with the big moment, his being drafted by a National Hockey League team. There was no doubt that the documentary would be of interest to a great many hockey lovers, since all of Eric's actions and gestures were already being examined under a microscope. I felt that a program like this might satisfy some people's curiosity. After my explanation, Carl asked some questions.

Q. And who will ensure the quality of the production?

A. I know several highly competent, very professional production companies in Toronto. It wouldn't be hard to interest one or another of them.

Q. What role would you play?

A. I would act as associate producer. Also, my participation would provide another definite advantage.

Q. Oh, what's that?

A. The production would be bilingual.

I thought this last detail would really capture his interest. I remembered that I had raised the question of French when I first met Eric; I also remembered that Eric had reacted positively when I teased him about it. The scene was still very vivid in my mind.

Q. Eric, did you know that there's one thing Gretzky can't do?

A. No, what?

Q. He can't speak a word of French.

A. Well, then, I will.

The offer I was making the Lindroses had a unique dimension. Not only would a high quality video be produced about Eric's last season in junior hockey, but more importantly, Eric would have the opportunity to learn a little French, bearing in mind that if he ended up in Quebec City or Montreal, he would be able to get along to some degree in the language of the majority. If he could speak some French, he would project a much more positive public image.

Carl Lindros's reaction to my proposal was less than enthusiastic. Without committing himself one way or the other, he promised to think about it and get back to me fairly soon.

Q. Is there anything else, Daniel?

A. Yes. We could also keep a diary and write a book to go with the video. The book would also be in both English and French.

Q. A book? What kind of book?

A. A kind of record, you know, just to satisfy the kids' curiosity.

When I mentioned the book, Carl said that the idea of a book had already been discussed by the clan, but they had not yet made a final decision in that regard. We continued to talk about various aspects of the proposal, and I returned to the language issue a number of times. I became very puzzled when I sensed that Carl Lindros had no interest at all in the issue which I considered crucial in the given context.

We finished our lunch and when I drove Carl back to work, he promised to get in touch with me in the coming weeks. As we shook hands, I asked him what he thought of the project in general.

A. I'm not sure. I'll tell you what. We'll all discuss it the way we always do in situations like this. Then I'll tell you what we think.

A few weeks went by before Carl contacted me. He telephoned one morning and we had a short and not very encouraging conversation.

Q. Well, what did you decide?

A. We think that, for the time being, Eric should keep his contacts with the outside world to a minimum.

Q. What do you mean by the outside world?

A. The media, the general public.

I knew then that the project had not received the support of the clan. Nevertheless, I tried one last time to interest Carl in the aspect of the project that was closest to my heart.

Q. And what about the French idea?

A. The possibility that Eric will live in Quebec City one day is almost non-existent. So let's leave it for now.

I was naive enough then to think that the Lindroses' decision was based on their belief that the Nordiques would not finish last that year. However, now that some time has passed, I owe it to myself to admit that Carl's answer contained a much more revealing message. By the fall of 1990, the Lindroses had already decided against the Quebec option for their super-talented son. Why else would they have thrown away such a wonderful opportunity to prepare Eric to adapt to a situation he might very well have to face?

I wish I could have talked to Eric that day; but it was becoming more and more obvious that, to reach Eric, you first had to go through his father. Everything is filtered. Eric receives only what the clan wants to let through.

I feel nostalgic when I remember the time that Eric, just 16 years old and still innocent and naive, told me that he would be happy to wear a Quebec Nordiques sweater one day. And that he would manage to speak French just because the challenge seemed so natural and easy to take up.

At that time you could still reach Eric.

That time is gone.

Gone forever.

Chapter 3
THE CANADA CUP

S ometimes you are lucky enough to be in the right place at the right time as Eric Lindros was in 1991 when he had the opportunity to play in the Canada Cup. His participation in that prestigious tournament not only gave him the chance to make his mark on the international scene, it attracted a lot of attention in his own country, which won the Cup again that year, giving him invaluable exposure just when it could do him the most good. Had the competition taken place the year before or the year after, he would have been forced to sit on the sidelines after the June draft, champing at the bit.

At the beginning, the mere fact that he had been invited to the Team Canada training camp was considered an achievement in itself. The invitation was issued at the direction of Alan Eagleson, the mastermind behind the tournament. Eagleson openly admitted at the time that he was still haunted by a very embarrassing incident that had occurred in 1984, in connection with a situation identical to the one involving Lindros in 1991.

Q. What happened in 1984?

A. I was convinced in 1984 not to invite Mario Lemieux because he was only 18 years old.

Q. Was it a bad decision?

A. Bad? You better believe it. I was stupid to let the management group of '84 persuade me of that. This boy — 18 years old — had set every record; he was a giant of a man, physically and in ability. In my opinion, he would have been a star on Team Canada.

You can find a lot to criticize in Alan Eagleson — you only have to read *Net Worth* to see that. He is, however, a man who is willing to acknowledge his mistakes, or at least some of them, and he has always been willing to take the blame for the 1984 blunder of not inviting Mario Lemieux to the Team Canada training camp.

Q. Did it teach you a lesson?

A. Absolutely. I wasn't about to see that happen again. I made it clear even before Mike Keenan was made general manager, that Eric Lindros would get an invitation to the training camp.

Q. Does that mean Eric was sure he would make the team?

A. I didn't guarantee Eric Lindros and his father a spot for Eric on the team. I gave him an opportunity.

The 1991 situation was 1984 all over again. As had been the case with Mario Lemieux, Eric Lindros was only 18 years old and had just finished a phenomenal junior hockey season. And perhaps even more than Mario had been at 18, Eric was considered an exceptionally talented player who had reached the stage w..ere he deserved to be included on the list of the country's best hockey players. There was therefore every reason to invite him to the Team Canada training camp to try out for the team.

Q. Did he agree to report to Keenan right away?

A. Yes. That's what I like about the young man. He could very easily have hidden behind the insurance curtain like many other players did. "Oh I don't want to put myself at risk . . . I don't want to be hurt . . . it would be awful if I was injured." This young man has "balls" and he put his "balls" on the line and he came through for me.

Q. Would you say that Eric met your expectations?

A. He not only made me look good, he made Mike Keenan look good and he made our team a better team.

Eagleson's invitation to Eric raised a general hue and cry. Among those who protested were individual journalists, established NHL players, and certain agents who were not shy about saying exactly what was on their minds.

Q. What argument did you hear most often against having Lindros on the Canadian team?

A. Two agents — one a close friend, Don Meehan — tore a strip off me in Switzerland for inviting an untried player who would take the spot of an NHLer.

Meehan was obviously speaking on behalf of his many clients. He represents close to a hundred active players, including Pat Lafontaine, who has become one of the richest players in the League since coming to Buffalo. However, Meehan and the other critics stopped objecting pretty quickly when they saw that Eric was indeed ready to take his place among Canada's most talented hockey players. In fact, all those who were at the training camp, the players as well as the various observers, were soon convinced by what they saw with their own eyes — that far from being out of place, Lindros was integrating quite naturally into the select group that Eagleson and Keenan had assembled.

The Team Canada training camp started at Maple Leaf Gardens in Toronto. To most of the regulars involved in this periodic tournament (1991 was the fifth time the event was held), the Toronto hockey shrine was a strange setting. The Gardens had not been used as a site for the Canada Cup since 1976, because the late Harold Ballard, owner of the Gardens and second only to God at the time, was vehemently opposed to it. He was convinced that the Soviets had no business being in Canada. By 1991, however, with a new management in place and Cliff Fletcher in charge, the narrow-mindedness that had characterized Ballard's twenty-year reign at the Gardens was no longer in evidence.

The players gathered for the first time on August 3 at the Westin Harbour Castle Hotel. The next day, they showed up at Maple Leaf Gardens to try on uniforms and equipment. At first, few journalists were around, and the players were particularly cooperative with everyone who wanted to talk to them. I happened to be there when Eric came in shortly after noon. Looking very serious, he quickly took his turn trying things on. He did not go unnoticed, to say the least. You would think that an 18-year-old newcomer would have felt out of place in that constellation of established stars who were among Canada's best. Not Eric. Indeed, you had the feeling that he was the one being looked at rather than the one doing the looking. And he seemed unaware of being watched and oblivious to the attention he was attracting. Searching for familiar faces, he sometimes nodded or said hello to someone he knew. We noticed each other as soon as he came into the pressroom, and we talked for a few minutes.

Q. Hi Eric, how are you today?
A. Great. And you?
Q. Not too bad, thank you. How do you feel?
A. Real good. It's unbelievable being here.

This was the Eric Lindros I remembered — courteous, sociable and friendly, if not exactly warm. He still had something about him that was ingenuous, sincere, even a little naive. The tone of the conversation could not have been more relaxed as we continued chatting.

Q. Is it pretty well what you expected?

A. Yes. Even better. It's like Christmas night when you're opening all your presents.

I should point out that there were lots of "presents", as Eric called them, especially with regard to clothing. Not that all those shirts and sweaters in the Canadian team colours represented much in financial terms, but their symbolic value was extremely high. Eric behaved just like any normal teenager faced with so many treats. More important than anything else, however, was the feeling that suddenly came over him that he was part of a select group of athletes, the elite of his sport.

That first meeting of the players invited to the Team Canada training camp ended with an optional practice. Not surprisingly, Eric was the first player on the ice, late in the afternoon, and for a few glorious minutes he had the rink all to himself. As he skated in the Gardens where so much hockey history has been made, it was easy to imagine how naturally proud and happy he must have felt. At that moment, Eric was impressive. It was a lovely sight to see.

There is sometimes a tendency to forget that a hockey player is first and foremost an artist on skates. That day, as Eric Lindros skated alone on the ice of Maple Leaf Gardens, he was athlete and artist rolled into one, a winning combination that has helped to make him the newest sensation in contemporary hockey.

A few minutes later, another member of the troop skated out on the ice. It turned out to be not just any player, but Dale Hawerchuck. Dale, like Eric, had also been seen as a potential impact player when he was still playing junior hockey. Although it took Hawerchuck longer than expected to fulfil his potential, that does not alter the fact that today he is one of Canada's hockey elite. He has an impressive record — more than one thousand points in close to eight hundred games in the NHL, nine years in Winnipeg and a season in Buffalo—and he is still going strong.

Hawerchuck and Lindros automatically started passing the puck back and forth, practising some of the drills routinely used in such circumstances. I was standing next to the boards beside the Leaf bench with a small group of journalists, and every now and again as Hawerchuck skated by us he would toss out a remark. After the first few passes, while Lindros was totally absorbed in his own world, Hawerchuck said out of the corner of his mouth, "The kid's not bad". Then, after the two of them had made a few more moves, he said, still keeping his voice down, "Can't deny it, the kid's got talent". Finally, the third time he skated past us, he called out enthusiastically for all to hear, "Keep an eye on this one, he's going to make the team!"

Thus, Hawerchuck needed only a few minutes to find out what a number of others already knew — Eric Lindros was no flash in the pan! At the beginning of the training camp, there were several people who said that Lindros was a long way from being guaranteed a place on the Canadian team. Within a few days, it became increasingly and inescapably obvious to virtually everyone that Eric Lindros not only deserved the invitation he had received but that he should certainly be put on the team.

Alan Eagleson knew what he was doing when he directed Mike Keenan, the general manager and head coach of Team Canada, to include two untouchables — Wayne Gretzky and Eric Lindros — on the list of players to be invited. But there was no way he could ever have imagined the extent to which, at the end of the tournament, the presence of the novice would turn out to be as crucial as that of the great master. Lindros and Gretzky, each in his own way, made a dazzling contribution to the success of the Canadian squad in that remarkable tournament.

Since the management of Team Canada had chosen to invite some fifty players to the training camp, the number of participants had to be reduced. The process is usually accomplished in two stages. The first series of cuts eliminated Joe Sakic, the Quebec Nordiques' number one player. In addition to causing considerable surprise, Mike Keenan's decision to cut Sakic triggered an inevitable comparison between the present star player of the Nordiques and their future hero, Eric Lindros. While the two parties involved refused to make any comment whatsoever on the issue, observers agreed that Sakic was not at all his usual self on the ice. He seemed disoriented and preoccupied, as if something was bothering him. That something was undoubtedly related to the presence of his young rival, who exerted a subtle but undeniable psychological effect on him. Lindros's physical strength has often been remarked, and with good reason — it enables him to dominate his opponents fairly easily. He apparently has the ability to dominate people mentally as well.

While everyone was talking about how astounded they were that Sakic had been eliminated, Vincent Damphousse was pleased to see that he had survived the first cut and was still in the running, despite the fact that he was said by some to lack aggressiveness, an important asset in Keenan's eyes. Damphousse, who was still playing for the Toronto Maple Leafs at the time, had already had a chance to train with Eric by the time I spoke with him.

Q. What struck you the most about Eric?
A. His maturity. I've never seen a young hockey player so much more mature than others his age.

It is not surprising that Vincent should be struck by that aspect of Eric's personality, since he himself was considered very mature for his age when he was still only a rookie in the NHL. It is interesting to note that Damphousse began his career in Toronto, the first Francophone in Maple Leaf history to be drafted in the first round (sixth overall). He adapted to his new surroundings and learned to speak English very quickly, and as a result, everyone thought highly of him — the players, the press and the general public.

Vincent Damphousse was following the example of most Quebec players who start their hockey careers in an English-speaking environment. Rather than waste time feeling sorry for himself, Damphousse made every possible effort to adapt to surroundings far removed from his own and to an organization not inclined to recognize the French fact. Shortly after Damphousse began to play for the Leafs, another Quebec player, Daniel Marois, joined the team. He too succeeded in assimilating into the organization. Félix Potvin and Yanic Perreault are two other highly praised young Francophones who belong to the Maple Leaf organization. They should be joining the Leafs in the near future and are adapting as well. All these players, to their great credit, are working very hard to become fluently bilingual.

And all this time, Eric Lindros has been bad-mouthing Quebec. In English.

But I digress. Let's get back to the training camp.

Eric Lindros astonished everyone with his exploits on the ice, and every day more and more people were beginning to think that he should be given a spot on the Canadian team. At the same time, the press was starting to show greater interest in him. Then something happened that was as surprising as it was unexpected. Lindros, probably caught off guard and unaccustomed to the presence of so many seasoned reporters around him, became talkative. He was obviously looking for allies and must have thought everyone would agree with him.

At the beginning of the training camp, it had been established that Eric would say nothing pertaining to possible negotiations with the Quebec Nordiques and that he would refer all questions on the matter to his agent, Rick Curran. Some members of the press, probably unaware of this tacit agreement, innocently brought up the subject with Eric one day and, to the great surprise of everyone present, he answered their questions.

In a very serious voice, Eric told his listeners what he really thought in terms that left no doubt at all about where he stood. What he said left more than one person in the room feeling stunned, flabbergasted and confused.

I know that was how I felt.

Whenever I had asked Eric in the past why he was reluctant to consider a career in Quebec, he always told me it was a question of economics. Now I was finding out, at the same time as my colleagues, that in reality the situation was much more complex, maybe even a little absurd. According to Eric, the Lindros clan firmly believed that living in Quebec City would expose him to certain risks. First, there were few if any endorsement opportunities for an English-speaking person. Second, the closed nature of a small, totally Francophone city would hamper his cultural development. And last but not least, the political situation made the prospect of a career in Quebec potentially dangerous.

Q. Well Eric, what's going to happen?

A. The Nordiques won't have any choice. They'll have to trade me.

Q. Where would you like to go?

A. I want to go where I can be happy.

This could have been Eric's theme song. Almost every time he made a statement concerning his future he repeated the phrase "**I want to go where Eric Lindros will be happy**". And then he would shrug his shoulders and in the same breath add the refrain "**Let's move on to bigger and better things**", the implication being that Quebec simply did not fit in with Eric's aspirations.

It is not too difficult to imagine the shock, mixed with dismay and disappointment, that most Quebec journalists felt when they heard Eric make those remarks. The next day, to be sure of what he had said, I went into the dressing room after the daily Team-Canada practice, with a microphone in my hand. As I had expected, some of the journalists were repeating the questions that Eric had been asked the day before.

Among my colleagues who were present were Guy Robillard of the Presse Canadienne, Pierre Durocher of the *Journal de Montréal* and Réjean Tremblay of *La Presse*. I can still see the four of us listening to the tape I had made of Eric's comments. As print journalists whose integrity has always been above reproach, they wanted to be absolutely sure that they were reporting Eric's exact words. There could be no doubt that Lindros had really said what we thought he had said.

Réjean Tremblay, for one, could not believe his ears.

Q. What should we make of all this?

R. I think he's just mixed up, poor kid.

Q. Weren't you saying just the other day that Eric only wanted to exercise his basic right of free choice?

R. Yes I was. But that was before he made those humiliating remarks about Quebec.

After several days of close contact with Eric Lindros, Réjean Tremblay was face to face with a reality he was not equipped to deal with. At the same time that he admired the enormous talent of a young hockey player, he saw himself grappling with someone who appeared to be very self-centred.

To help Tremblay get a better picture of the Lindros clan, I suggested he talk to Eric's parents, whom he had not yet met. In the back of my mind, I was hoping that the Lindroses might use such a meeting to tone down their son's remarks a little. The occasion presented itself one Thursday evening at the Gardens, after the game against Sweden. As usual, Carl and Bonnie Lindros were waiting for Eric near the team dressing room. I took the opportunity to go up to Carl, and after we had gone through the usual greetings, I introduced Réjean to Eric's father. As the three of us stood there talking and laughing, Eric came barging out of the room. There was nothing particularly elegant about the scene that followed.

Eric's manner could not have been more cavalier. Without stopping to acknowledge us, he called his father over. Then, without saying a word to either of us, the two of them walked away and left us standing there while they had a private, whispered conversation. After a few minutes they headed back in our direction. Eric walked right by us without a word, and joined his mother and some friends. Carl resumed his conversation with us, but he avoided looking us in the eye and had trouble hiding his impatience. Réjean Tremblay simply could not get over it. We started to discuss what had happened.

Q. I wonder what Eric could possibly have said to him.

A. It's very simple Daniel. He told him not to trust me.

Q. Come on, Réjean, you're being paranoid. What reason would the Lindroses have to be on their guard?

A. Take my word for it, Daniel. I have no doubt that Eric told his father all about me and warned him to watch what he said.

As time went by, I came to share Réjean Tremblay's view of the incident. The Lindroses have gradually become more and more reserved around Francophone journalists, and their attitude towards the press in general has deteriorated as well. There have been a great many instances where members of the Lindros clan have treated members of the press with suspicion, and even contempt.

A little earlier the same day, a small, revealing incident had occurred in the Team Canada dressing room that showed another side of Eric Lindros.

A friend of mine, Véronique Morin, a former journalist in the Toronto newsroom of Radio-Canada, arrived late in the morning to prepare a report on Eric's earlier statements. She was doing freelance work at the time and her employer on that particular occasion was Télé-Métropole in Montreal. She had with her a cameraman named Gail, who was a veteran of the Toronto sports scene and a regular around the Gardens. When Gail Mugford saw me, he asked me to give Véronique a hand and familiarize her with the way things were usually done in such circumstances. Naturally, I said I would.

It is a well-known fact that a woman's presence in a male dressing room elicits a certain amount of comment. In Véronique's case, it would be fair to say that her presence would not go unnoticed in a female dressing room either. She is a warm, engaging person who attracts attention wherever she goes.

On this occasion, unaccustomed as she was to the world of male dressing rooms, Véronique was not feeling completely comfortable. She told me that she had already said hello to Eric Lindros and that he had seemed rather cold and distant.

After doing what I could to help put Véronique more at ease in going about the work she had to do, I went over to Eric and told him that she just wanted to ask him a few short questions, nothing to worry about, and asked him to cooperate with her.

He then asked me, "Do you know her well?"

I said, "Yes, Eric, but you should know that she's not a sports reporter, so she's a bit nervous."

To this, Eric immediately retorted without thinking:

"I don't care, she's dumb!"

Eric is of course not the only person to think women don't know much about sports. Most athletes, however, keep their opinions to themselves or make veiled comments when they are talking among themselves, away from cameras and microphones.

Besides, Véronique was quite aware of the stir her presence was causing and, given the circumstances, was showing a great deal of discretion, confining herself to the business at hand. When she asked me if it would be all right for her to speak to Wayne Gretzky, I told her to go ahead, since I knew very well that the Great One was used to such situations. She also interviewed Eric Desjardins of the Montreal Canadiens, who behaved like a perfect gentleman. It goes without saying that when the interview was over, Desjardins was bombarded on all sides by the other players, calling him a "lucky dog" wanting to know who the "babe" was he had just been talking to.

Russ Courtnall, also from the Canadiens, looked especially curious . . .

As for Eric Lindros, the episode revealed another side of his character, perhaps not the nicest, but nevertheless part of the overall picture.

A clearer and more complete picture of Eric began to emerge as events unfolded during the rest of that week. Comments kept streaming in from everywhere concerning the sensational statements attributed to Eric, and you could sense the tension around him. Several journalists were reluctant to approach him, some openly admitting that they dreaded having to face the young player.

Since the start of the training camp, I had conducted only one official interview with Eric, and that was during the first few days of the camp, when there was no suggestion of controversy over Quebec. Now, a Radio-Canada public affairs program was showing a high priority interest in the Lindroses. I told the program's chief editor that I would be glad to approach Eric and try to convince him to do an in-depth interview in which he would have a chance not only to state his opinions, but also to discuss other subjects that interested him. I caught Eric late one afternoon as the dressing room was gradually emptying out, and since he had a free moment, I talked to him about the project. You could sense that he was beginning to get fed up with the whole Quebec story and that he wanted to turn the page on what had been a painful first chapter in his career.

Q. You look tired, Eric.

A. Not really, I'd just like to be finished with this whole business.

Q. Exactly what I was going to talk you about. I have a favour to ask. I'm sure you know that everybody in Quebec has been talking about you since you made those statements. The Radio-Canada show "Le Point" would like to give you a chance to talk about it and wants me to do the interview. Would you be willing to answer some questions?

A. That depends on what you're going to ask me.

Wanting to make him feel less wary and more secure, I did what journalists usually do in such circumstances — I tossed the ball back to him:

Q. What approach would you suggest for the program?

A. Why not do it from the point of view we were talking about yesterday?

Eric was recalling a remark he had liked, which had been made the day before in the course of a conversation we had had about the philosophical aspects of the issue.

Q. You mean the question of human rights?

A. Yes. All I want is the basic right to choose where I live my life.

The conversation he was referring to was unquestionably one of the most interesting we have ever had. We had talked of this and that, and I had mentioned to Eric that his conduct over the last few days had reminded me of the character played by James Dean, the hero of post-war teenagers, in *Rebel Without A Cause*, the first of his three films. Imagine my surprise when he replied with great seriousness:

A. I know, except in my case I'm fighting for a cause.

Q. Oh? What cause?

A. The cause of everyone who wants the right to choose when it comes to making important decisions.

Eric is definitely not a stupid young man. In terms of his intellect, he must have a pretty high I.Q., and he seems to have a fairly wide general knowledge as well, especially with regard to movies.

I assured him that we would do the program from the point of view he had suggested and asked him again if he would do the show for Radio-Canada.

A. Yes, I'll talk to you.

Q. Is it O.K. with you if we wait till the week-end?

A. Sure, whatever you like.

Given the climate surrounding Eric's presence on Team Canada, the end of the week was shaping up to be particularly exciting. On Saturday, Canada would be playing Czechoslovakia in the Montreal Forum, and on the following Monday, the Soviets would face off against Team Canada at Le Colisée in Quebec City.

Armed with Eric's promise, I arranged to tape the interview at Le Colisée Sunday at noon, after the team practice. It would never have occurred to me in a million years to suspect that things might not go as planned.

First, to the Montreal Forum.

A light work-out was held Saturday morning, as is usual on the day of a game. The fact that large numbers of observers were milling around did not faze those who were used to being involved in this type of competition. At the end of the practice, in keeping with tradition, journalists were allowed into the dressing room, although the team coaches and public relations people did seem more on edge than usual.

Eric Lindros was now more than ever the centre of attention, but here too he was watched from a distance. Very few people went up to talk to him. There were, of course, one or two journalists who tried to engage him in conversation, but the exchanges were short and routine.

At one point, when I saw that he had a moment to himself, I went over to say hello. I could see that he was more nervous than he usually is before a game. It was obviously not the time to start a long, involved conversation, so I just gave him a quick reminder of the next day's schedule.

Q. Is tomorrow's interview still on?

A. I don't think so. Mike (Keenan) doesn't want me to give any more interviews.

Q. But Eric, you gave me your word.

A. Well, it's O.K. with me, but maybe you'd better check with Bill.

The Bill he was referring to was Bill Tuele, head of public relations for the tournament and an old hand. Bill had been working for the Edmonton Oilers for ages and had had some great years in the Gretzky era. He was used to tense situations and knew how to cope with requests from even the most persistent of people. So I went to see him and asked him to approve of my plan to interview Eric.

Q. Bill, you have to let us interview Eric tomorrow.

A. Listen Daniel, it was Mike who gave the instructions. If it was just up to me, I'd tell you to go ahead.

Q. What should I do then?

A. Let me talk to Mike — but it won't be easy.

Bill then went into Mike Keenan's office. As I waited impatiently in a corner of the dressing room, I watched the little drama unfold before me. Eric was summoned to the manager's office. He was in there for less than five minutes. When he came out he went straight over to his bench without speaking to me. A few minutes later, Bill Tuele appeared and reported that the policy was still the same — no interviews at Le Colisée the next day with any journalist no matter who, just a press conference after the morning practice.

Q. What went on in the office, Bill?

A. Not much. But Eric agrees with Mike.

Q. Did he mention that he gave me his promise?

A. Yes he did, but he said he thought you had put him on the spot and that you had intimidated him.

To think that I had intimidated the intimidating Eric Lindros! You can imagine how surprised I was. I had never had the slightest inkling that Eric had felt forced to talk to me, nor had I ever received any indication from him that he did not want to be interviewed for the French-language network of Radio-Canada. Something must have happened in the interim—but what? Mike Keenan is not a man who is easily contradicted, so it is more than likely that the directive came from him. However, from what is known about the Lindroses, it is hard not to conclude that they must have been aware of the decision.

What was most revealing about the episode, which was full of inconsistencies, was that Eric had not been frank with me.

The press conference took place at Le Colisée the next day as planned, with all the attendant noise and commotion that was to be expected.

The game between Czechoslovakia and Canada gave Lindros the chance to show that he could function under the most severe conditions, which on that occasion took the form of playing under a barrage of boos and catcalls. The crowd in the Montreal Forum wanted to let him know what they thought of the inflammatory remarks he had made about Quebec from his home base in Toronto. Although hockey fans are best known for showing wild, mindless enthusiasm for their heroes, when faced with a stand they found unacceptable they reacted strongly and unequivocally. Lindros, however, kept his cool. He played a remarkable game on the ice and then went on to give an outstanding performance at the post-game press conference. Eric had thus won a moral victory and successfully made it through the first stage of his journey on Quebec soil.

After the conference, I stationed myself near Carl and Bonnie, both of whom were visibly more nervous than before. They were standing near a half-drawn curtain waiting for their son to join them, as he had been doing after every game since the beginning of the tournament. Bonnie, who was usually rather cool to journalists, said hello to me first and, to my great surprise, started to talk to me in an almost friendly tone of voice. After a few minutes of small talk, I turned to leave so that the Lindroses could have a few moments of privacy with their son. I said good-bye to Carl and told Bonnie that I hoped she would enjoy the rest of her stay in Quebec. We parted on the following note:

Q. Not too many problems so far, Bonnie. I hope you'll enjoy your visit to Quebec City.

A. I don't know, Daniel. We haven't decided yet whether we're going to Quebec City on Monday. One thing's for sure, we're going to stay in Montreal tomorrow to think things over.

Q. Why the hesitation? Won't Eric need your support more than ever?

A. You're probably right. But he's the one who suggested that we shouldn't come. He's afraid we'll get hurt.

Q. Do you think he has reason to be afraid?

A. You better believe it. We have received death threats!

I could not believe my ears! But when Bonnie Lindros had confided the information to me, she certainly did not sound like she was making it up. Besides, given the circumstances, her disclosure was quite believable.

Preoccupied with these rather sombre thoughts, I walked over to the pressroom to sound out a few of my colleagues and see if I could get a reading on the situation. It was late, close to midnight maybe. Most correspondents were supposed to be finished working, especially the newspaper journalists, who have a very tight deadline, particularly on Saturday nights.

As I reached the floor where the pressroom is located, I happened to bump into Pierre Durocher of the *Journal de Montréal*. We started talking about the game for a few minutes and, inevitably, the Lindros's name came up.

Q. What's your opinion of the crowd's reaction, Pierre?

A. It could have been worse.

Q. Yes, but is it an omen for Monday in Quebec City?

A. Maybe it won't be so bad. We'll see.

Pierre's comments confirmed my first impression of him — he was not the type to overdramatize and he seemed to have good judgment. I decided to tell him what Bonnie Lindros had just told me.

Q. I just spoke to the Lindroses, Pierre. Bonnie told me they've had death threats made against them.

A. What? Are you sure?

Q. Of course I'm sure. Do you want me to repeat her exact words?

A. You bet.

Q. "We have received death threats." Just like that.

A. That's no joke. I'm going to call the *Journal.* Maybe there's still time to include the news in tomorrow morning's edition.

Q. Gently with that story, O.K.?

A. Don't worry. Just a short paragraph.

Some publications are often accused of catering to sensationalism, and the *Journal de Montréal* certainly has that reputation. So I must admit I was very surprised to see that this was not the way the paper handled the death threats story. Its professionalism in this case was no doubt due to the sense of moderation and sound judgment shown by a colleague on a night when some others might have been inclined to push the panic button . . .

On the same day, *The Toronto Sun*, Toronto's equivalent to the *Journal de Montréal*, came out with the following headline on Page One:

"FAN PUNCHES LINDROS"

The headline alluded to an altercation that had apparently occurred as Lindros was leaving the Forum, in which blows were exchanged between him and a discontented fan. The headline was no doubt intended to give the impression that people in Quebec were using violence against the young hero. In referring to the rather heated controversy involving Lindros and the Nordiques, certain Toronto journalists have occasionally accused their Quebec colleagues of showing a lack of restraint in their handling of the story and of using excessive language to inflame their readers. The day *The Toronto Sun* ran that headline, the accusers should have admitted that they were guiltier of those charges than the people they were accusing.

In the next few days events moved towards a climax. In less than 48 hours, Eric's mettle would be tested. He not only had to face the Soviets, a major challenge in itself, he also had to undergo that intense experience under adverse conditions, since the game was being played at Le Colisée de Québec.

There was a particularly impressive turnout on the part of the media at the first Team Canada practice on Sunday at Le Colisée. While the players were going through a routine work-out on the ice, tongues were wagging away up in the stands. Everyone, but everyone, was speculating on how the crowd would behave during the game against the Soviets the next day.

It felt good to be in Quebec City. Although I was born in Quebec, I have had to live and work elsewhere in Canada for the last twenty years. As some of my English-speaking colleagues and I sat around talking, memories from my past began to come back to me, and one of my colleagues, Don Chevrier, also began to recall some of his experiences in Quebec. Don Chevrier is not a name normally associated with hockey. He is a veteran television sportscaster whose main field is baseball, although he does have some connections to professional boxing. He does the play by play commentary for the Toronto Blue Jay games and, because of his expertise and ability, is often asked to appear on the American networks as well. Chevrier was going to be doing the play by play for the upcoming game against the Soviets on the CTV network and he confided to me that he was somewhat worried about how the crowd in Quebec City was going to behave.

Q. What do you expect tomorrow?

A. I really don't know. I just hope it won't be ugly.

Q. Do you intend to speak about Lindros in detail?

A. I don't see how I can avoid it. I think the human aspect should be emphasized — remember, he's only an eighteen-year-old kid even if he does have exceptional potential.

Chevrier, like several other English-language journalists, has been careful not to compromise himself in this whole story, which is beginning to look more and more like a clash between two cultures. Although there is a general sense of uneasiness with regard to Eric's comments, Chevrier and other veterans of the sports scene have been quick to forgive Lindros for taking the stand he did. Indeed, many of them have advised against reading too much into the whole situation, putting Lindros's behaviour down to inexperience and impatience in the face of a complex situation.

Jim Proudfoot of *The Toronto Star*, who was sitting next to me, was unable to resist adding his comments to those of the others. Proudfoot is a columnist and longtime member of the press corps, extremely knowledgeable and conscientious. Our paths have often crossed over the years, and I enjoy talking with him. We may not always see eye to eye, but whenever we bump into each other it is quite natural for us to start a conversation. Proudfoot has definite opinions about the Lindros case, and has aligned himself with those who agree with Eric.

Q. So, you agree with Eric's position?

A. On the whole, yes. And I find the reactions in Quebec far too negative.

Q. Well Jim, they are really hurt. After all, what Lindros is saying amounts to rejection pure and simple. And no one likes to feel rejected, right?

A. You people in Quebec are funny. You yell that you want your own country, but at the same time you don't like it if someone tells you he's not interested in coming to live there.

The conversation continued on a cordial note. To take the edge off what he had just said, Jim started singing the praises of Quebec City the way so many other English-speaking Canadians do, using the usual clichés such as "it's a great place to visit".

Shortly afterwards, the journalists began to leave the stands of Le Colisée and make their way to the room where Lindros was going to hold the press conference. The numerous production teams had already set up their equipment. The number of microphones and cameras bordered on the ridiculous — you would have thought the entire world was waiting to hear the words a young hockey player was getting ready to utter.

It was a long time before Eric appeared. He finally came in, with Bill Tuele at his side, and took his place at the centre of the table. A minute later he was facing a barrage of questions.

Eric maintained throughout the conference that he would definitely not be coming to Quebec to further his career. He gave economics as the main reason for his decision, but said that there were cultural, political and social factors involved as well.

Although nothing new emerged from that rather painful exercise, it should be noted that a convinced young man showed that he was determined to fight to the finish to achieve his ends.

What is really worth remembering is the way things started happening whenever Eric was around. The next day, for instance, after the morning practice, the following incident occurred.

Journalists invaded Eric's corner of the Team Canada dressing room from all sides, hoping to get an exclusive shot or a sensational statement. They insisted on waiting for him while he took a shower. Suddenly Bill Tuele appeared and announced in his booming voice, "Sorry guys, Eric left by the back door."

Unfortunately for Bill, Eric's clothes were still there and everyone could see them. Naturally, someone asked, "Did he go out naked?" Bill could hardly resist the general laughter that followed, and conceded, "Well, I guess he's still around."

Noting that the journalists had relaxed their guard for a moment, Bill quickly scooped up Eric's clothes and took them out of the room. When the film crews realized that there was no point in waiting around any longer, they began leaving the premises. After a while, there was no one left in Eric's corner of the dressing room.

Eric finally appeared quite a bit later, surrounded by impressive looking bodyguards. He pushed his way through the room and made straight for the exit as fast as he could. He looked scared to death.

Eric Lindros was afraid of Quebec, no question about it.

During the episode, Wayne Gretzky was standing near the door of the dressing room talking to two or three reporters who were still there. It was all very strange.

We had just seen and heard, in a rather distressing event, the future star of Canada's national sport make it plain that he was only doing what was right for Eric. Now we were hearing words of quite another kind, in a completely different tone, from a player considered by a number of people to be the preeminent active hockey player today. Someone asked Wayne what he thought of it all.

A. I think that professional sports are changing more and more, and that we are heading into a climate where players will be making tougher demands.

Q. And what do you think will happen to Eric?

A. He'll probably get what he wants. He's got too much talent for them to ignore him.

If there is one thing everyone agrees on regarding the Canada Cup, it is that Wayne Gretzky turned in an exceptional performance, not only during the games but in the practices as well. Number 99 had shown many times before that he deserves all the accolades usually associated with his playing, both as an individual player and as a member of his team. His renown is due at least in part to the fact that he strengthens any team he plays with. Wayne Gretzky's talent is universally recognized.

For my part, my contact with Gretzky over the years has always been characterized by courtesy and mutual respect, even though much of it occurred in circumstances that were very emotional. For example, I was in Los Angeles to see him play his first game for the Kings and I was in Edmonton when he returned to the Northlands Coliseum to play against his former team-mates and fans. I also saw Team Canada win its historic victory over the Soviets in Hamilton in 1987 when, in the final minute of the game, Wayne Gretzky and Mario Lemieux combined to score the memorable goal that gave the Canadian team the Cup. I will never forget the touching scene of Mario and Wayne hugging each other for the Radio-Canada camera. It was an eloquent picture — our country's two greatest hockey players of the 1980's, one from French-speaking Canada and the other from English-speaking Canada, sharing one of the greatest moments in their careers. Both men later said that the experience had given them the opportunity to play the best hockey they had ever played in their lives.

On each of these occasions, Gretzky was completely open and cooperated in any way he could. Over the years, whenever he has been asked what he thinks about the inevitable comparisons between him and Mario, he has always replied that he is honoured to be considered as talented as his rival.

Eric Lindros has responded very differently, I remember, when he was asked a similar type of question. He replied that he did not like to be compared with anyone else, saying ''I'm not a Wayne Gretzky, I'm not a Mario Lemieux, I'm just Eric Lindros''.

The only player Lindros is willing to be associated with is Mark Messier, for the simple reason that he likes the rugged style of play of Gretzky's old team-mate.

Eric Lindros is no ordinary hockey player and we might as well get used to him. He goes his own way and likes doing as he pleases. Nothing fazes him, on or off the ice. The long and the short of it is that Lindros plays hockey because he loves the game and wants to be successful at it.

To return to the Canada Cup . . .

At the long-awaited game against the Soviets in Quebec City the next day, everything went well. The crowd's behaviour was more than appropriate, and Eric's playing was equal to the expectations of those who believed in his incredible talent. He got the first goal for Team Canada in a game that ended in a 3-3 tie.

After the game, there was another press conference with journalists sitting and standing wall to wall. This time Mike Keenan spoke first, and when it came time to yield the floor to Number 88, Mike remarked, ''Go easy on him. He's only eighteen.''

You don't have to worry Mike. The kid may be only eighteen, but he knows how to defend himself. In fact, he may even take a malicious pleasure in being part of such a controversial story, especially since he has been the author of it.

That press conference, like the others before it, went off smoothly. It was even a little repetitive — both questions and answers were becoming redundant.

You almost felt like calling out ''Let's move on to other things'', as Eric has sometimes suggested.

Well, at least we now know where we stand.

Chapter 4

MEDIA REACTION

"LET LINDROS SIT THERE TILL HE ROTS"

That was the headline run by *Le Journal de Montréal* on Tuesday, August 13, 1991. It seems to be the theme Quebec journalists have most frequently repeated in writing about the Lindros saga. During the same period in Toronto, on the other hand, no journalist has even once suggested the alternative of leaving Lindros in hockey limbo. Indeed, journalists in Ontario have all agreed that the Nordiques should trade Lindros as soon as possible. Thus if you take the opinions of the sports writers as definitive, Quebec and Ontario have taken opposite sides in this controversy.

Of the journalists in Quebec, Bertrand Raymond of the *Journal de Montréal* seems to have been the most realistic since the beginning of this complex debate. He does not always reveal his sources, but whoever they are, they have often helped him zero in on the facts by furnishing him with valuable information. Raymond realized very early on that the Nordiques were facing an impossible task. Still, however clearly he foresaw the outcome of the issue, he has continued to believe that the Nordiques should let Lindros cool his heels for as long as it takes, and he has not hesitated to say so.

The Toronto press keep criticizing their Quebec counterparts for allowing their emotions to overcome their judgment in this story. But Raymond's article of August 13 creates just the opposite impression because he presents such a well-reasoned, coherent argument. He begins with the premise that the Nordiques have a responsibility to their public. He then points out that the Nordiques have been put in an unfair and untenable position through no fault of their own. The fact is that American teams have a clear advantage over Canadian teams because the U.S. dollar is worth more and because there are far more tax shelters in the United States. It is obvious that the Lindros clan are making full use of these very real circumstances to rationalize their absolute refusal to consider the Quebec option. Raymond concludes with this perceptive comment: "It is becoming more and more obvious that Eric Lindros has no intention whatsoever of negotiating with the Nordiques."

Bertrand Raymond has followed the development of the story very closely and has made a commendable effort to try to understand the Lindroses' thinking. They, in turn, showed that they trusted him to some degree by allowing him to spend a week-end with them in early September during the Canada Cup tournament, at the time of the highly publicized games against Czechoslovakia at the Montreal Forum and the USSR at Le Colisée de Québec.

The first-hand knowledge Raymond gained from that experience has convinced him that, in refusing to negotiate with the Nordiques in any way, the Lindros clan has been motivated first and foremost by the language issue. Another factor is the almost pathological aversion Bonnie and Carl have to Marcel Aubut, president of the Nordiques. From his conversations with the Lindroses, Raymond has come to the conclusion that their distrust of Marcel Aubut goes deep.

I have to admit that Bertrand Raymond has been right about this complicated case all along. A statement he made on June 23, when it was still possible to hope, shows that he was amazingly astute from the start. He said then that "Until such time as the issue is resolved, the Lindros case will remain so explosive that it could blow up in the faces of the Nordiques and the National Hockey League at any time".

As Christmas approached, Bertrand Raymond became more and more convinced that the Lindros clan was going to come out on top in the case.

Q. What do you think comes out of this whole story?

A. The Lindroses are going to prove once again that they are stronger. With Bonnie in charge, the Lindroses managed to run the Ontario Hockey League and they're about to try the same thing with the National Hockey League.

Q. How do you answer the charges made against you by your Toronto colleagues that you and other Quebec journalists are lacking in critical judgement?

A. I would tell them to take a good look at their own articles! When Mario Lemieux didn't sit down at the table with the Pittsburgh Penguins[5], the Quebec press criticized him. Has the Ontario press published a single negative comment about Lindros yet?

---

5 In June 1984, Mario Lemieux, Pittsburgh Penguins' first choice, had refused to come to the team's negotiating table at the time of the draft. He chose to stay in the stands at the Montreal Forum, claiming that he did not have to shake hands with the Penguin managers as long as no agreement had been reached between the two parties.

Q. Not that I know of. Does that prove anything?

A. It sure does. The Toronto press lit into Mario Lemieux and treated him like dirt all through his first three or four seasons in the NHL. At least we were honest enough to tell Mario he had acted badly and I remember that at the time we wrote that he had received bad advice. Can you tell me why they think everything Eric Lindros does is great?

Bertrand Raymond was not the only journalist doing good work for the *Journal de Montréal*. Pierre Durocher also provided first-class news coverage, especially during the Canada Cup. On September 5, Durocher wrote an excellent article on some rather presumptuous comments Eric had made about the political climate in Quebec, in which Lindros went so far as to make some questionable comparisons between Montreal and Quebec City.

Unfortunately, the same newspaper had the bad taste to print a column by Bernard Brisset in which the author's choice of language is highly offensive. It is hard to give anyone credit for his opinion when he expresses it by using obscenities to make his point. Brisset deals with the subject again on December 2 and again his vocabulary is scathing, but this time he stays within the bounds of propriety, so that you can follow his argument. Once you realize what he is really saying, you can see that he is right — "enough is enough". After expressing his disgust at hearing Lindros speak, Brisset goes right to the heart of his argument, saying that Lindros is the hero in combat, leader of the cause. He claims that Lindros represents those in English Canada who want to put Quebec in its place. It is hard to contradict Bernard Brisset when he says that the Lindros case no longer involves the Nordiques alone, but also all of Quebec, a conclusion that provides food for thought. Jim Proudfoot of *The Toronto Star* takes malicious pleasure in using Brisset to illustrate what he refers to as the uncalled-for and unacceptable journalism of some of his Quebec counterparts.

Jim Proudfoot is not a man to mince words when it comes time to take sides in a controversial story. This is especially true in the Lindros case. Jim has strong views not only about the issue itself but also about why journalists in Ontario and Quebec have taken two such different approaches to the story.

Q. How do you explain the obvious differences between the coverage in Ontario as compared with that in Quebec?

A. It's emotional in Quebec. It's certainly not emotional here. I can only speak for myself, but there is no emotion involved on my part. I think I've been able to look at it objectively.

Q. Can you give me an example of where the Quebec journalists have been over emotional?

A. A hockey player doesn't want to play for their team, for God's sake. Why is that an insult? Here you have a province that has been telling us for ten years that it's separate from Canada, that it's a foreign country. Then someone says, "I don't want to go and play hockey in that foreign country". Then they're insulted. They say, "It's an insult. We've been insulted". So now they're trying to protect the Canadian Olympic team from the corrupting presence of this — in my mind — outstanding individual who is willing to play for the Olympic Team. So now we have Quebec, or people in Quebec, individuals in Quebec, taking on this added stance that they're suddenly interested in our Olympic team. Where does this sudden interest come from? I mean, we're supposed to be professional journalists. We're not Croatians and Serbians. We're not Ukraine trying to break away from some evil empire. We're supposed to be intelligent people. It seems to me these guys are acting like children.

Jim got a little wound up when he made the above comments, and I just let him go on, trying to keep the microphone in front of him as he started moving his head to emphasize his arguments. He must have noticed me smiling a little from time to time, because he suddenly stopped and said:

"As a matter of fact, I probably sound as though I'm becoming emotional."

I was in fact discovering a Jim Proudfoot I hadn't known existed. With his emotional outburst, he became guilty of the same offence he has accused his Quebec colleagues of committing.

In an article written at the beginning of November, Proudfoot said that the "Lindros fiasco" could sooner or later mean the death of the Nordiques. He based that ominous statement on two very specific premises. First, it will be impossible for the team to survive without building a new arena, and Lindros is the key to that project. Second, the Nordiques have lost all credibility among their supporters by losing game after game, season after season. He ends by predicting that ultimately, the Nordiques will move or perish.

Q. As far as I know, you're the only one who's made such discouraging predictions.

A. That's been implied in many of the things that Marcel Aubut has said. Without a new arena the Nordiques franchise will die and Lindros is central to that plan. Lindros would be the key to an arena project; accordingly, if they don't have Lindros there's no arena and without an arena there's no Quebec Nordiques. That's my rationale, Daniel.

Proudfoot repeats his view of the facts with conviction, insisting that it is based on an objective analysis of the situation.

Without realizing it, Proudfoot has fallen under Eric Lindros's spell, which he has cast over most of the journalists in Toronto. At the beginning of December, the Canadian Olympic team spent a few days in Ontario and Jim Proudfoot had the opportunity to cover their game against the Americans in Kitchener. Lindros was there, of course, and his performance completely enthralled the veteran sportswriter.

Q. What do you mean by "The Eric Lindros factor dominates any analysis of the 1992 Olympic hockey tournament"?

A. Big Number 88 makes Team Canada a force to be reckoned with for a change, even feared. The snickering has ceased. It has been replaced by profound respect, thanks to this one individual.

The *Toronto Star*, the daily paper Proudfoot works for, has by far the largest circulation of any English-language newspaper in Canada, selling 500,000 copies during the week and 750,000 on Saturday. Any journalist with a by-line in the paper has to be considered fortunate and successful. In 1991, the sports section of the *Star* was enriched by the addition of Bob McKenzie, a first-class columnist and former editor of the well-known weekly, *The Hockey News*. McKenzie enjoys a reputation for unrivalled competence in his field.

While he was still with *The Hockey News*, McKenzie had said it was highly unlikely that Lindros would ever play for the Nordiques. What he based that assertion on, he alone knows. It is possible, however, to believe that, as a result of his close contacts with the members of the Lindros clan, he had access to privileged information. Rick Curran, Eric's agent, counts McKenzie among his friends. The columnist even lives in Curran's old house, which he moved into when Curran left Toronto to take up permanent residence in Philadelphia.

The above situation in no way alters the fact that McKenzie's work as a journalist is excellent. His articles are always interesting and more often than not they shed light on events related to the world of hockey.

With regard to the Lindros story, you have to trust that McKenzie has penetrated Eric's world. The best example of this was the follow-up to the disclosure of the now-famous 50-million-dollar offer that the Nordiques had apparently made to Eric .

McKenzie was the only journalist who was able to get Eric's reaction to the disclosure. *The Toronto Sun* had been the first to break the story which took more than a few people by surprise and created a sensation when it appeared under the by-line of Scott Morrison on the morning of Saturday November 16. The next morning, *The Sunday Star* stole the limelight from *The Sun* with McKenzie's article. McKenzie had managed to talk to Eric on Saturday evening, just after he had returned from his long hard tour of Europe with the Canadian Olympic team. Without a shadow of a doubt, that article shows more clearly than any other how torn and confused the young idol was in his thinking. First, McKenzie confirms the rumours that Eric Lindros is seriously considering quitting hockey for a year in the event that the Nordiques refuse to give in to his request to be traded. When asked why he has made this decision, Eric admits that:

"It's vindictive".

Apparently, Eric Lindros considers it an insult to be offered a contract that could be worth up to 50 million dollars. That must be why he wants to punish the people who insulted him, why he wants to stand up to those who are trying to spoil him with all that money, by threatening to retire from the scene until his name becomes available for the 1993 draft.

When McKenzie says, "That ain't news, folks, it's reality", you have to believe him since he heard it right from Lindros himself, with whom he has a good relationship. The moral of the story, according to the writer of this extremely troubling article, is obvious—no matter how much money the Nordiques offer, the decision has been made. Eric Lindros is not going to Quebec City.

While *The Toronto Star* relies on Bob McKenzie's articles to get the facts in the Lindros story, *The Toronto Sun* depends on the work of Scott Morrison. We have to bear in mind that the two papers aim at very different readerships. *The Sun* is a tabloid, published only in the morning, while *The Star* publishes several editions a day. Furthermore, the bulk of the general information in *The Sun* focuses on the sensational, placing the emphasis on provocative headlines and pictures with shock value, and its most popular page is page 3, with its picture of the Sunshine Girl.

Like the rest of the paper, the sports section uses attention-grabbing headlines, and its columnists, especially James Hunt and Steve Simmons, often take unequivocal stands which colour the content of their articles.

James Hunt is one of the regular veterans of the Toronto sports scene. He is well-known and, in his own way, well-respected. Everyone is fully aware that although good old Hunt makes a lot of noise, his bark is worse than his bite. Every Tuesday morning Hunt writes an opinion column, expressing ideas that are as varied as they are sometimes preposterous. In one of these columns, he asks Marcel Aubut a hypothetical question:

"Suppose Eric Lindros had called the Quebec Nordiques' bluff and accepted their 50-million dollar contract offer. Where would the Nordiques have got the money?"

Hunt answers the question himself, saying that "NHL officials are kidding themselves if they think they can play in the same financial league as the NBA, NFL, and Major League Baseball. The difference is the other leagues all have multi-million-dollar TV contracts with major American networks. Hockey has to try and make do with a pittance from the Sports Channel. They better find out in a hurry you can't buy champagne with a beer budget."

Here again, it is worth noting that Hunt's message, "Suppose Eric Lindros had called the Quebec Nordiques' bluff", is remarkably similar to the one the Lindros clan has been sending.

The Lindroses assume that Marcel Aubut, the villain of the piece, is setting a trap for their naive and innocent son. And Hunt, despite his maturity and years of experience, has swallowed the Lindros logic whole, as if he were a green young reporter. But their reasoning—the Nordiques are offering a fabulous contract; the Nordiques don't have the money; therefore it's a trick—is merely an example of false logic.

Scott Morrison has a lot more credibility. He was the one who got the famous scoop about the 50 million dollars, and his approach all along has been to look at the facts rather than the rumours. Nevertheless, like his colleagues in Toronto, he does not hide the fact that he has totally accepted the Lindroses' position.

Q. Why do you approve of Eric's attitude?

A. Because he's one of a handful of players that come along over the years that are in the position — a Gretzky would be in a similar position, a Lemieux — that they can call their shots. They're a very special few.

Q. Do you think he and his family did the right thing in trying to achieve their purpose?

A. From the very beginning they were at least up front with Quebec and told them this all along. The one thing you've got to give them credit for, whether you agree or disagree with their stand, is that they were up front right from the start with the Nordiques —even before the draft; so you can't ask for any more than that, I don't think.

It is not surprising that Morrison has only good things to say about Eric, since their relationship has developed on common ground. Eric does not feel at all threatened by the Toronto columnist who has consistently described his achievements in glowing terms. Morrison says that he was won over by Eric's manners the first time they met.

...our first meeting go?

... up to me and introduced himself to me and we got a very good relationship in terms of talking. He's a mature kid — at times he still shows that he's a kid — but I think he has handled himself very well in the comments he's made. I think, under the pressure of people calling from all sides, he handled it quite well.

Writing about Dave Chambers shortly after he was fired as coach of the Nordiques in mid-November, Morrison took the opportunity to criticize the Nordiques for not having helped Chambers by trading Lindros. In the same breath, he added the following:

"It [the Lindros situation] is the source of the twisted emotions and distorted thinking in the media and public."

In all justice to Morrison, I must say that he realizes it is normal for people to get worked up in a city where the frustration level is high.

Q. What do you mean by "normal"?

A. If this guy was holding out on the Leafs, you'd see stories every day about it.

Q. Don't you believe that emotions are stronger in Quebec?

A. Traditionally the media in that province are far more emotional than in other areas. They've always been regarded — the Montreal media, the Quebec media — as being far tougher on teams than they have to be and that sort of thing. I do think that it [the Lindros case] has gotten out of hand.

Morrison may not admit it, but he sometimes lets his feelings get in his way in his assessment of the facts. An obvious example of this occurred on December 11, 1991, the day after Team-Canada played the Canadiens in the Montreal Forum. Morrison reported that the jeers which greeted Eric each time he came out on the ice were "more forced than heartfelt."

How can a journalist know what motivates a crowd to boo, I wonder. Clearly, Morrison does not want to acknowledge that the message sent by that particular group of fans was sincere and genuinely felt. In his view, "All that was genuine was a look of relief afterward on Eric's face."

Further on in the column, Morrison returns to the subject. Without batting an eyelid, he claims that if people booed, "It was because they felt obliged to, which confirms the Lindros affair is not a provincial calamity after all, but instead a twisted regional issue. And it's difficult to know whether the wrath in Quebec City is as strong among fans as it is in the media."

Not only in the wonderful world of sports do Quebec journalists have the reputation for being so emotional.

In her weekly *Globe and Mail* column, "Quebec Voices", (December 10, 1991), Pauline Couture reports that ". . . journalists' feelings about nationalism are a hot topic in Quebec. In its convention magazine, *La Fédération professionnelle des journalistes du Québec* set up a debate, and an article by Alain Saulnier, a producer at Radio-Canada's "*Le Point*", says that both anglophone and francophone journalists seem to think francophone nationalism is emotional and out of line, while English-Canadian nationalism is 'more reasonable, more rational . . .'"

This prejudiced view does not hold up under analysis. You just have to speak to the majority of English-speaking sports writers in Toronto to realize that they too get emotional about events that directly affect them. Lindros is the perfect embodiment of the contemporary anglo-saxon mentality. It is therefore perfectly natural that in taking a stand, he has struck a chord in the so-called rational journalists in Toronto. Of course, more often than not these journalists try to give the impression that they are above sentimentality. Nevertheless, when they are confronted with really profound questions, most allow themselves to be much more spontaneous and therefore more sincere in their writing.

One Toronto columnist who does not hesitate to say what he thinks is Steve Simmons. You will find this out soon enough if you so much as mention the CFL to this ardent defender of American football, which is his specialty. Since he writes mostly about football, Steve Simmons has not really had a chance to write about the Lindros saga in any detail. When I asked him to share his opinions on the subject, he responded eagerly.

Q. What do you think about the overall situation?

A. The situation? I think it's gotten out of hand, more than anything else. It's just at a stage where both sides have their backs to the wall and logic was lost somewhere.

Q. What strategy do you think should have been used?

A. I think there was a simple solution and both sides missed it.

Q. What was that?

A. Sign a one and one, sign a one-year contract with a one-year option. He would have been a free agent after two years; he would have had his money; he would have been out of there. Quebec would have had a chance to maybe get their building started. I think both sides have lost here. Nobody's winning right now.

Q. What do you think of Eric as a person?

A. I feel sorry for Eric in some ways, because I think Eric wants to play hockey in the NHL and this must be hard for him. Sometimes I don't think the words that come out of Eric's mouth are Eric's words. I think someone has told Eric this, whether it be his mother, his agent, his lawyer, whoever. If you ask him the same question a week later that you asked him the week before, you get the same answer. It's like you trigger a mechanism: that's the answer to that question. There is no natural response.

You have to admire the lucidity of Simmons' argument. After all, he has been around sports for years, rubbing shoulders with the greatest names in American football and baseball. One of the things for which Eric is criticized in a number of circles is that he thinks he is "bigger than the game", that he is as it were, above it all.

Q. Do you share that point of view?

A. Well he does, and maybe he is.

Asked about the coverage by the Toronto media, Steve Simmons offers a surprisingly clear-sighted analysis.

Q. Is Eric Lindros getting preferential treatment?

A. Toronto has been protective of Eric Lindros. If anything, we've been on his side. I don't necessarily think that's always been right, but Toronto has definitely been protective of Lindros and very few people have been critical of him, taken shots at him or called him 'baby' or 'whiner' or anything else. The amazing thing about him or the whole story is that it's captivated so many people.

William Houston of *The Globe and Mail* is one of the few Toronto newspaper columnists who has dared to write articles that do not always praise the Lindros clan. In his column "Truth and Rumours", Houston writes about fact and fiction in the sports world. From time to time, he has made some revealing observations not found elsewhere with regard to the Lindros case. He has, more often that not, made unflattering comments about Bonnie Lindros.

Q. Where do you get your information?

A. The information is there. Lots of people have access to it, but most don't seem to pay attention.

Q. How do you explain that?

A. That's easy. The Lindroses upset people and some journalists are afraid of the consequences. They don't want to run the risk of breaking their ties with them or upsetting them. Don't forget that Lindros is likely to be news for years to come.

Q. Aren't you afraid of the Lindroses' reaction?

A. Not really, except that I have to be careful, especially when Bonnie is involved. I could be accused of harassment if I reveal everything I learn about her.

If few journalists have the guts Houston does, it is partly because he is one of a small group of journalists who are virtually unassailable. A few years ago he wrote a biography — unauthorized, of course — of the late Harold Ballard and incurred the wrath of the colourful former owner of the Toronto Maple Leafs. When Ballard got wind of Houston's intentions, he threatened to slit the writer's throat if he went ahead with the project. Despite the threats, the book was published. It should be read by anyone interested in the excessive involvement a megalomaniac like the deceased magnate of the Leafs could have at a certain period.[6]

Other members of the English-speaking press besides those in Toronto have followed developments in the Lindros story. Newspaper people

---

6 Houston, William, *Ballard*, McLelland and Stewart–Bantam Ltd., Seal Books, Toronto, 1985.

in every large city in the country have offered their own bits of wisdom and have tried to penetrate the mystery behind the phenomenon. It is worthwhile to spend a minute looking at the coverage given to the story by *The Gazette*, the only English-language daily in Montreal. Since the paper is comparatively far removed from the Lindros clan, it does not have to worry about how its members will react, which is probably one reason why it has been able to side with those who would like to see Eric reach an agreement with the Nordiques. In a very interesting article on the subject, Pat Hickey supports Marcel Aubut. In line with the position taken by the hockey establishment, Hickey bases his argument on the fact that Eric's attitude puts the integrity of the sport in jeopardy.

"The integrity of the draft system is at stake, and if athletes are permitted to make a mockery of the system with outrageous demands that force teams to trade them, the draft is rendered useless."

It is to Hickey's credit that he is completely objective in analyzing the situation. Hickey ends the article on a very serious note.

". . . if players are allowed to dictate where they want to play, teams like the Nordiques won't be able to sign quality players at any price."

A month later, Hickey addresses the subject again. In this article he manages to refute one of the crucial arguments used by the Lindroses in refusing to consider Quebec City for Eric—their claim that endorsement opportunities in the Quebec market are virtually non-existent. Hickey coolly analyses the situation and concludes that an athlete's marketability depends on three considerations: personality, talent and market. Lindros's personality is outstanding, his talent unequalled and as for publicity-generated revenue, the Quebec market, as we learn in the article, is second only to New York's in the NHL.

Red Fisher is the chief hockey writer for *The Gazette*. The veteran journalist does not hold back when talking about Eric Lindros.

Q. What do you think of Eric's attitude?

A. I think he was dead wrong in what he did. Like all the other players who want to play in the National League, he should have made up his mind to follow the rules. Otherwise he should get into another business.

Q. Why do you think he took the stand he did?

A. His family, the advice he's getting. I don't really blame him because he's only 18. I think he's got some terrible advice.

Since this opinion is not at all in keeping with that of Fisher's English-language counterparts in Toronto, it is strange, to say the least, to hear him express it in such explicit and unequivocal terms. It seems that in Toronto Eric's behaviour has gained almost universal approval, whereas in Montreal it has been called into question. Perhaps this irrefutable difference stems from an underlying cause that is neither linguistic nor cultural.

Perhaps it is political.

In covering the Lindros affair, *The Gazette* has also been fortunate to have Michael Farber. He writes as a reporter rather than as an analyst, but he does it well, in an extremely polished style. Farber has a sense of humour all his own, and it is refreshing to read something about Eric Lindros that makes you smile rather than shrug or, even worse, feel like lashing out at someone.

Although the *Journal de Montréal* has done a good job in covering this story, the same cannot be said for *La Presse*, the other large French-language daily in Montreal. For one thing, there was very little coverage at the beginning. Except for a few routine articles at the time of the June draft in Buffalo, no attempt was made to look at the subject in depth until August, when Philippe Cantin launched the first attack. However, evaluating his comments as a whole is not easy, because they really are just comments. He insists on spouting opinions and impressions that are clearly his own. The problem with this kind of approach is that he ends up sticking his neck out, and although he shows some courage in his analyses, he often misses the point.

At first, Cantin had rather positive feelings about Eric Lindros and thus his opinions were favourable. The day after the Buffalo draft — which he watched on T.V.! — Cantin came to the defence of the young hero in an article that was really bizarre, not because it was somewhat sympathetic to Eric but because it was full of strange remarks from beginning to end.

The strangest has Cantin asking "what crime the young man has committed to be judged so severely by both the media and the public". Then on September 6, Cantin says that he himself will not "miss" Lindros, accuses him of being "stubborn as a mule", adds that we should "feel sorry for him", and then describes Eric simply as a "poor kid".

With Cantin, it's all or nothing. Either he is right on the mark or he misses the target entirely. In August he is brilliant. On the 14th, he shows that the Lindros clan is playing politics, and on the 16th, he reports that the Lindroses' demands are a reflection of the way professional sports are changing.

When he starts making predictions, however, don't bet on him! On August 19, he writes an article entitled, "Lindros in Albertville? Not likely . . ." And on August 21, at the end of an article about Carl Lindros, he says, "Don't be surprised if, after all the controversy, Lindros puts on a Nordiques sweater in time for the first game of the season". He could hardly be more wrong.

When Cantin is at his best, however, he is a pleasure to read. On Friday, September 6, in an article entitled, "When they support Lindros's crusade, Gretzky and Yzerman are playing a dangerous game", Cantin asks a series of pertinent questions that reflect both his insight and the careful thought that he has given the matter. And sometimes Philippe Cantin has a sense of humour which is quite delicious.

If you think Philippe Cantin is way off base with his rather hasty predictions, wait until you read what Michel Blanchard writes on September 5. According to him, "Eric will never have the nerve to return to Oshawa."

In the article called "Eric Lindros's bluff", Blanchard predicts that "Lindros will wind up in the NHL next year wearing a powder blue sweater with a fleur-de-lis across the chest."

It is definitely not *La Presse*'s year for accurate predictions!

Fortunately, the newspaper has also had Réjean Tremblay's input, although it could have benefited from more of it. Tremblay does not begin to address the Lindros affair until the Canada Cup Tournament, but when he does, he indicates his appreciation of the drama to come:

"People will remember 1990 as the summer of the Indians, but 1991 will be the summer of Eric Lindros."

Those first words of Tremblay on the subject show how well he understands the magnitude of the situation. The article is well worth reading in its entirety because it offers so much food for thought. A brilliant analysis of the situation, it is lucid, comprehensive and incisive.

Tremblay says, "the Eric Lindros case (. . .) is a symptom of the illness affecting a country, an economy and a society, which are losing the ability to be competitive."

When he refers to the fact that Lindros wants to be able to choose where he is going to work, Tremblay touches on the heart of the problem and says, in all honesty, that "Eric simply wants to exercise his basic right to sell his services to the highest bidder".

Further on, in discussing another crucial factor, namely the financial aspect of this complex tale, he comes to the conclusion that hockey teams in Canada may have to look to the government for assistance.

"It would not be the first time an industry with financial difficulties has done this."

From the beginning, Eric Lindros has been described as an impact player. Tremblay believes that Eric Lindros is giving a new meaning to the word "impact" and that some day "the Lindros effect" may well be a topic for discussion in learned treatises on political economy.

A week later, Tremblay begins to see the whole story more clearly, but it is unlikely that his conclusions about this new phenomenon of modern hockey will offer any comfort, even to the most optimistic of fans. He finds "so many contradictions".

Réjean Tremblay can appear to be a little nasty at times, but if you get beyond his choice of imagery, you can hardly help agreeing with his conclusion.

"I get the feeling that Eric Lindros has a swelled head, so filled with his own importance that he cannot understand anything else."

Needless to say, Tremblay has gotten into trouble as a result of his views. The family, following Bonnie Lindros's lead, has apparently threatened to sue *La Presse* for defamation. However, it is debatable whether Tremblay's implication that Lindros is narrow-minded and self-centred actually constitutes defamation. It should also be pointed out that it does not take much to make Bonnie Lindros feel threatened.

Tremblay does not hesitate to face the political aspect of the Lindros debate head on. Here again, his argument is logically expressed.

"The Lindros case is easy to understand, all black Americans would understand it. It is not a question of respect but of contempt. (. . .) As long as Quebec is part of Canada, and as long as Canada wants to continue to exist in its present state no matter what the cost, then this province whose people are looked down on are supposed to worship an idol who has been openly contemptuous of something that is the very essence of Quebec. The country is sick, not Eric."

These courageous remarks were made two days after the September 10 exhibition game between the Canada Cup team and the Montreal Canadiens at the Forum in Montreal. It was a confrontation between opponents with almost the same name, the Canadiens and the Canadian.

It was also a confrontation between a man and a people, at the end of which there was no winner, although both sides had restated their positions in no uncertain terms. The people booed the man who rejected them. And the man, through his behaviour, attitude and language, showed his self-centred arrogance and his contempt for the people.

The most moving, true-to-life and disturbing article to appear in *La Presse* was written by Chantal Gilbert the day after the Team-Canada–Canadiens confrontation at the Forum in Montreal where Lindros had been subjected to the incessant boos of the crowd. Chantal Gilbert's article reflects the strong emotions she felt at the time, filtered through her keen intelligence and distinctive personal experiences.

The title of the Gilbert article asks the question, "How does it feel to be detested by a people?" The subtitle clearly states what the writer thinks about the subject: "MISTER LINDROS DESERVED THE BOOS . . ."

Gilbert's response to the question in the title is intuitive: "For Lindros, it doesn't seem to be a problem. He just ignores it. He lives in his own world, follows his own rules and does his own thing. For Lindros, other people simply don't exist."

Chantal Gilbert ends the article on a reflective note, speculating on how Lindros's behaviour may affect the future of hockey.

"It saddens me to think of all the little boys (. . .) who see him making a farce of the NHL rules, controlling the climate of the game with his whims, scorning a city and a people. All these little boys will grow up one day. If they follow Lindros's example, even partially, the NHL is in real trouble. Just imagine a lot of little Lindroses in the NHL and on the streets. What a nightmare! Worst of all would be all the Lindros mothers in the stands. I can't bear to think about it."

It is easy to imagine how members of the Toronto press would react to Gilbert's article. Instead of recognizing it for the gem it is, they would probably accuse her of letting her emotions get the better of her judgement, and in this case they would probably be right. But is it so terrible to speak from the soul?

We should appreciate Gilbert's article for what it is, a cry from the heart that helps us to understand the far-reaching implications of the issue.

* * *

As far back as we can remember, no athlete from English Canada has been the subject of so much discussion in the city of Quebec as Eric Lindros. It is not hard to understand why. The Nordiques are Quebec City's only professional team, and as such, they are naturally a symbol of the city's pride. When you attack the Nordiques, or hold them up to ridicule, the pain is felt by all the people of Quebec. No wonder the daily papers continue to feature stories about the Lindros affair.

One of the deans of the sports pages in Quebec City is Claude Larochelle, who has been writing for *Le Soleil* forever. From the beginning, the ups and downs of the Lindros saga must have given this writer some moments of intense anxiety, because his good nature, sense of honour and professional integrity are such a basic part of him. If there is any sports writer who deserves to be called an honest man, in the philosophical sense of the word, it is Claude Larochelle.

To say that Larochelle appears naive may be misleading. He is straight-forward and decent; he is no fool. He expresses his own opinions and ideas right up front, and gives the impression that he trusts others to do the same.

It is therefore not surprising that, in an article published on May 4, 1991, Larochelle says, "Eric Lindros's mom is well-disposed towards Quebec", adding that, in a long telephone conversation with her, he has learned the Lindroses have nothing against Quebec. He quotes Bonnie as saying that "the Francophone aspect of Quebec City (. . .) is not a problem".

A week later, Larochelle tells us that Eric "feels at home in la Vieille Capitale" and that he has no problem with "the climate, the language, the culture or any other aspect of Quebec City."

In June, Larochelle is still saying as sincerely as ever, "The young phenomenon is certainly not resisting Quebec, and it's not a question of language, either".

An article three days after the June draft in Buffalo finds Larochelle continuing to maintain that "The Lindros clan has nothing against Quebec City".

Two months later, the front page of *Le Soleil* carried an exclusive by Claude Larochelle, stating that Lindros was asking more than three million dollars a year. A scoop with such far-reaching implications was quite a coup for the seasoned journalist, but unfortunately for him, a number of other reporters claimed that Marcel Aubut had leaked the news, taking advantage of Larochelle's naivité to get a reaction from the Lindros clan. The next day, good old Claude again shows himself to be an innocent, when he ends an article with the words, "The negotiations will be difficult, but everything will be settled in November."

Larochelle was still sticking with his story that the Lindroses liked Quebec City. On August 26, in an article entitled "Two philosophies clash", he says, "I have never noticed the least opposition to the city of Quebec", then ends with the prediction "It's going to happen!" In other words, Larochelle clearly believed that the two parties would come to an agreement.

On September 11, Larochelle began to face a few facts. It was only a start, but in an article published the day after the famous game between Canada and the USSR at Le Colisée de Québec, the veteran journalist writes, as if he has just discovered what most people already know, that the Lindros clan still thinks it can dictate policy to the NHL.

A week later, Larochelle is repeating his old line. "All this fuss [about sponsors coming to Quebec] and we don't even know if Lindros will ultimately report to the owners of the fleurs-de-lis at the beginning of October, although *I still think he will.*"

On September 28, Claude Larochelle opened his eyes long enough to notice that "Eric Lindros is still giving Quebec the cold shoulder". But he must have closed them again, because he continues with a statement that shows his failure to see that the Lindroses don't want anything to do with Quebec: "Eric is careful to add that he has nothing against Francophones".

In order to be clear in my own mind about his opinions, I telephoned Claude Larochelle and spoke to him for over an hour. With great difficulty, an embarrassed Larochelle admitted that, like just about everyone else, he was finally beginning to realize that the Lindroses, led by Bonnie, saw Quebec as hostile and dangerous as far as Eric was concerned.

Q. How did you finally come to the conclusion everyone else seems to have reached — that Eric and his family don't want to have anything to do with Quebec?

A. It's just the feeling I get after reading everything written about them and hearing what's being said everywhere. I realize that they are prejudiced against Quebec City.

Q. At this time [Friday, December 13, 1991], what do you think about the whole thing?

A. Eric will never play here. A couple of weeks ago I told Marcel Aubut to trade him.

Larochelle does not usually throw in the towel so easily; on the contrary, it takes a lot to get him to change his mind. But even he can no longer deny the facts, and he does not want to have anything more to do with the Lindroses. When I told him that the English-language press in Toronto has accused Francophone journalists in Quebec, especially in Quebec City, of going overboard in their reporting and being too emotional in their approach, he raised his voice.

A. Our English language colleagues can get just as emotional as any of us in Quebec.

Q. Do you have an example of that?

A. The day after the draft in Buffalo, *The Toronto Sun* attacked Quebec in a provocative article which, for no apparent reason, accused us of fostering Francophobia.

The article in question was by Dave Fuller, who was trying to illustrate the problems English-speaking people are likely to face if they have to earn their living in Quebec City. To prove his point, Fuller relied on the testimony of two people — Clint Malarchuk, an English-speaking Canadian, and Claude Loiselle, a Francophone. Malarchuk said he had had a fairly successful stay in Quebec City, but that he didn't wish the experience on other English-speaking Canadians. Loiselle said quite openly that his experience with the Nordiques had left him bitter, especially after some negative comments he had made about the Nordiques were used to give his parents a hard time. Fuller concluded that Quebec City was isolated from the rest of North America.

Eric is awarded the Canadian Junior Hockey Player of the Year trophy at the Memorial Cup awards night in Quebec City on May 13, 1991. CANAPRESS Photo Service (Jacques Boissinot)

Eric hoists the Memorial Cup into the air after his team the Oshawa Generals clinched the title defeating the Kitchener Rangers 4–3 in double overtime in Hamilton on May 13, 1990. CANAPRESS Photo Service (Steve McKinley)

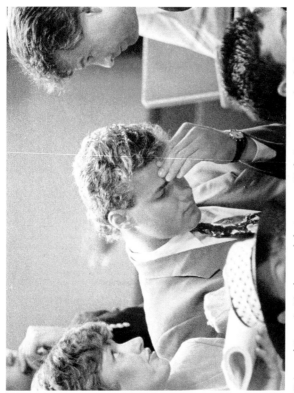

Eric and Bonnie Lindros and their agent Rick Curran ponder their next move after Eric was selected by the Quebec Nordiques during the NHL entry draft. Eric has yet to sign a contract. CANAPRESS Photo Service (Hans Deryk)

▽ *After being selected first overall in the 1991 NHL entry draft Eric greets various members of the Quebec Nordiques organization with a Nordiques jersey in hand. CANAPRESS Photo Service (Hans Deryk)*

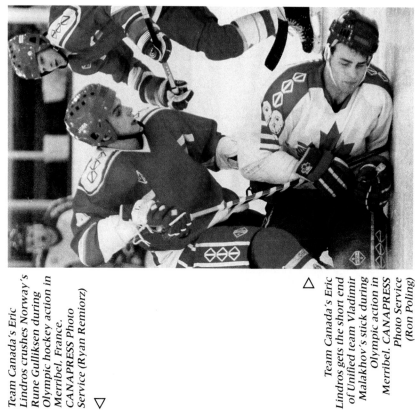

Team Canada's Eric Lindros crushes Norway's Rune Gulliksen during Olympic hockey action in Merribel, France. CANAPRESS Photo Service (Ryan Remiorz)

Team Canada's Eric Lindros gets the short end of Unified team Vladimir Malakhov's stick during Olympic action in Merribel. CANAPRESS Photo Service (Ron Poling)

Team Canada's Eric Lindros slides the puck past German goaltender Helmut De Raaf in an overtime shootout in Olympic quarter final hockey action in Merribel. CANAPRESS Photo Service (Ryan Remiorz)

Team Canada's Eric Eric Lindros celebrates after scoring his second goal of the game against Switzerland during 2nd period Olympic hockey action in Merribel. CANAPRESS Photo Service (Ryan Remiorz)

Team Canada's players (L–R) Sean Burke, Gordon Hynes, Eric Lindros and Kent Manderville show their disappointment as they wait for the medal ceremony following their 3–1 loss to the Unified team in Olympic competition in Merribel. CANAPRESS Photo Service (Jacques Boissinot)

△

▽

Team Canada's Eric Lindros is congratulated by an Olympic official after losing to the Unified team and being awarded an Olympic silver medal in Merribel. CANAPRESS Photo Service (Ryan Remiorz)

Team Canada poses for a team photo after winning the silver medal in the Olympic hockey final in Merribel. CANAPRESS Photo Service (Ron Poling)

Hockey legend Gordie Howe (right) shakes hands with junior superstar Eric Lindros (left) at a hockey clinic sponsored by The Sports Network in Toronto. CANAPRESS Photo Service

Junior hockey superstar Eric Lindros attempts to do it all as he dons a Toronto Blue Jays uniform and tries out for the team. The most ballyhooed junior hockey player since Mario Lemieux and Wayne Gretzky has all the prerequisites for a dazzling pro career. Globe and Mail

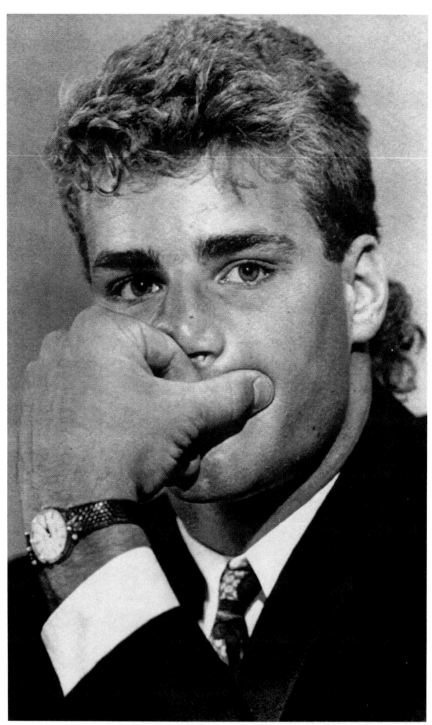

Eric Lindros in quiet contemplation. Associated Press (Mike Groll)

At this point in the conversation, Claude Larochelle did a complete about face with regard to the Lindros story, and even went so far as to add the following:

A. For once, the Québécois are all together. They feel they've been insulted but nobody has been taken in. When Lindros said he would play in Montreal but not in Quebec City, he took us for a bunch of suckers. Everybody saw through his game — he expected to gain allies in Montreal to back him up against us in Quebec City. But he was sorely mistaken—he brought us together instead.

As we were saying goodbye, I could hear that Larochelle sounded unhappy. He came back to the subject without being prompted, as if he somehow needed to express his thoughts more clearly.

A. My opinion has sure changed. I think that something, somewhere has turned the Lindroses against Quebec, but I have no idea what it can be. They really are prejudiced against Quebec, and I no longer see why the Nordiques should persist in going after a player who feels like that.

Other journalists whose articles about Eric Lindros have appeared in the sports pages of *Le Soleil* include Maurice Dumas, Kevin Johnston and Yves Poulin. Johnston and Poulin usually do straight reporting, but Dumas is more of a columnist. He seemed to see through the Lindroses right from the start. He did not mince words, when he said in May, "Lindros is still tied to his mother's apron strings". In June the message was "Lindros is too greedy", and in September he called Lindros "conceited, arrogant and contemptuous".

Q. You've been saying for a long time that Lindros will never play for the Nordiques in Quebec City. What do you base your statement on?

A. I've been saying that since April 1991, because Lindros has never had a good word to say about Quebec, not even before he was drafted, not even before the end of the season. I don't want to boast, or say I told you so, but I did see through his game very quickly.

Dumas is really offended when he hears that English-speaking journalists in Toronto have accused their Quebec counterparts of being blinded by their emotions.

A. The Francophone press didn't get vicious until after the Canada Cup tournament, that is, after the Lindros clan fired the first volley by making references to separatism.

Q. Did that justify what the press did?

A. The arrogance and contempt shown by the Lindros clan, led by Eric, was unacceptable. When I say the Lindros clan, I'm excluding Rick Curran, Eric's agent. All through the controversy, Curran has just done what he was told in order to protect his commission. After all, if a negotiating agent has a client like Eric, he really doesn't need any others.

Q. So the Toronto press is wrong about Quebec journalists?

A. Absolutely. But don't forget that they see Quebec City as a small town.

More often than not, the darts thrown at journalists in Quebec City by those in the Queen City have been aimed at Claude Bédard, who writes for the *Journal de Québec*. Bédard incurred the wrath of some of his Toronto colleagues, mainly because of his crusade to boycott the game between the Olympic team and the Nordiques at Le Colisée in Quebec City in December. Eric had arranged to be absent for that game, a tactic which was not appreciated by hockey fans in the area.

When you study what Bédard has written on the subject since the spring of 1991, you have to admit that he really showed insight and restraint throughout the whole affair. At the end of an article published on May 15, a month before the draft, Bédard mentions that Eric's parents "are most reluctant to see their son come to Quebec City". Bédard saw the truth long before anybody else.

A few weeks later, on June 3, in a serious, positive and encouraging article, Bédard analyses the impact Eric is likely to have on the team, both on and off the ice, when he joins the Nordiques. Bédard says that "Lindros and the Nordiques are waging a war of nerves", and ends on a note of suspense: "The two parties are getting ready to do battle".

The tension felt by the Lindroses mounted steadily as the date of the draft drew nearer. Realizing this, Claude Bédard tactfully told his readers:

"Without saying so out loud, the Lindros clan is just as anxious as the Nordiques clan. No one knows for sure what step to take next. And the family of the new young hockey hero is beginning to lose face."

Everything finally came to a head in Buffalo, causing Bédard to go all out to unravel the Lindros mystery and write, "It's all settled. Eric Lindros will not be playing hockey in Quebec City." The next day he added, "Controversy is in the air, and the battle between the clans is about to begin".

In August, Bédard wrote some articles to keep readers up-to-date on the latest developments. Then, on September 6, he made a direct attack on Jim Proudfoot for saying that the Nordiques would be honouring their commitment to the National Hockey League by giving another team a chance to get their hands on Lindros. Bédard says:

"With all due respect for Jim Proudfoot, whom I have known for more than twenty years, I have to say that he is absolutely wrong."

The article Bédard wrote the day before the long-awaited game between the Soviets and the Canadians at Le Colisée is called "Lindros is beginning to find himself in a jam". The day after the game, Bédard paid homage to the Quebec fans who behaved so well during the game. The following day, he offered a clear, accurate analysis: "A barely polite welcome interspersed with boos from the crowd will not mollify the Lindros clan. Nothing has changed. Things are still at an impasse."

Although I have read everything Bédard has written about the Lindros story over and over again to see what prompted the Toronto press to make accusations against him, I have not found anything inappropriate or inconsistent in his choice of language. His arguments have followed the rules of logic and he has complied with the most basic journalistic standards. He reports the facts, supports them with corroborative statements and testimony, and draws sound, reasonable conclusions based on the evidence presented.

Albert Ladouceur, a colleague of Claude Bédard, is quick to come to his defence when given the chance.

Q. Do you think Claude has gone too far?

A. No, just the opposite. Of all those who have been in a position to make their views known, Claude has been one of the most level-headed for a long time. When the story started to escalate, Claude decided to stand up and say what he believed. Besides, he may be the only journalist who still believes that Lindros will end up in Quebec City. Claude still thinks the Nordiques and the Lindros clan are going to come to an agreement in the end.

This may be one time when the two Claudes—Larochelle and Bédard —actually have something in common. Both men seem to be naive enough to believe in the possibility of a fairy-tale ending in which everyone lives happily ever after.

Sports writers are not the only members of the media who have had something to say about the Lindros case. Some editorial writers have tried to come to grips with the issues as well, although not many have succeeded.

In "Eric in the land of dragons", Raymond Giroux of *Le Soleil* asks, "Why are we devoting so much time to this rather ridiculous case?" He then answers his own question: "Because the Lindros story has gone beyond the boundaries of sports." He goes so far as to say that "all of Canada is talking about nothing but Eric Lindros". After a few comments about the political aspects of the debate, he accuses Lindros of having started it all himself with claims he made in *Maclean's* magazine. Giroux reminds us that "Politics and sports have never mixed". Further on, he expresses his idea more clearly "Professional sports depend on a stable political climate for their survival". Giroux ends his editorial with another question which he answers himself:

"How can anyone seriously imagine putting the burden of a political and linguistic tragedy on the shoulders of a young man who has only recently reached the voting age and probably doesn't have a clue about the drama that is being played out in his name? Enough, already!"

The *Maclean's* article referred to by Raymond Giroux should be read more than once, because author Bruce Wallace lets Eric speak for himself. Here, probably for the first time, Eric Lindros has clearly stated in no uncertain terms that he does not think the Quebec option is worth considering.

"Sometimes, you have to look at the political aspect of the thing, (. . .) If things are not going well politically in a certain climate, then you have to think twice about whether you want to be there."[7]

The author of this very revealing article is quite right when he comments, "By citing political reasons for his refusal to join the Nordiques, Lindros may provoke a backlash that extends beyond the hockey world. (. . .) In refusing to report to Quebec while making it known that he would be willing to play in Toronto, he (Lindros) runs the risk of becoming a symbol of the growing tensions between Quebec and the rest of Canada."

Bruce Wallace did an excellent job in preparing this article, considering that he had very little time to do it in and that, in order to interview Eric, he had to negotiate with both the Lindros clan and Team Canada, neither of which is easy to approach or to satisfy.

Q. What were some of the issues you faced in doing this story?

A. The Lindroses were mad about a lot of things. They were upset at the fact that the interview had even occurred. They were upset that Curran had not been involved. It was Team Canada that arranged the interview and there was a lot of fuss about who would be in control and how I even got access to Eric.

Q. How do you know all that?

A. Bonnie made sure I knew she was not only annoyed at me and *Maclean's*, she was also annoyed at Team Canada for what she considered to be exploiting Eric.

Q. Why didn't you mention any of this in the article?

A. Bonnie didn't want to be quoted in the story.

---

7 Wallace, Bruce, "Lucky Lindros", *Maclean's*, Vol. 10, No. 36, September 9, 1991, pp. 34, 37.

Q. Why not?

A. She said she causes Eric enough trouble when she speaks.

Wallace has a lot to say about his experience with the Lindroses. Like most people who have had to deal with Eric's parents, Bruce Wallace remembers very clearly how difficult it was to satisfy their demands. Eric himself was quite cooperative during the interview, although he did not always find it easy to express his thoughts. As a result, Wallace was unable to include some of Eric's comments in his article.

Q. Can you give me an example?

A. Eric mentioned an article that someone had showed him from *The Toronto Star* referring to the number of English-speaking people from Montreal who wanted to leave Quebec.

Q. Why didn't you include this in your story?

A. He said "Those are people who were born there and grew up there and they want to leave. Why are people giving me such a hard time for not wanting to go there?" It was a quote that should have been in the article, but he did not express it very clearly and it was difficult to include.

Bruce Wallace wanted me to know that he was originally from Quebec and that he is bilingual — his French is more than adequate. He also said the article was never intended to give only the Lindroses' point of view.

Q. Then why didn't you meet with the Nordiques?

A. I tried, but the only spokesperson I reached was Guy Lafleur, and he was not officially speaking for the Nordiques.

Q. What is your overall impression of this experience?

A. I find the whole story fascinating. It's two groups of people that just don't communicate.

Q. Would you say they are totally incompatible?

A. Absolutely. It's the meeting of the two solitudes.

Wallace says he knows Aubut quite well since he has done stories about him.

Q. What is your impression of Aubut?

A. I understand his mannerisms and what he's accomplished and how proud of it he is. He tried to communicate that to the Lindros family.

Q. What did they say?

A. They don't see it like that at all. There's a whole lot of miscommunication where the two sides don't understand one another.

Q. Does Marcel Aubut know that?

A. No, my frustration was that Aubut and the Nordiques would not return my calls.

Since Carl Lindros had told me the clan had reacted negatively to the *Maclean's* article, I mentioned this to Wallace as we ended our conversation.

Q. The Lindroses didn't seem to like your article, Bruce.

A. I know. They hated it.

Q. Does that bother you?

A. No. Actually, it's a good sign.

Three months after Bruce Wallace's article appeared in *Maclean's*, *Chatelaine* ran an article by Kate Fillion about Eric Lindros. Since both magazines are published by Maclean Hunter, the two articles use the same appealing photographs, which are the excellent work of Rick Chard.

The pictures, however, are the only thing the two articles have in common. While Bruce Wallace gives us some insight into the minds of the Lindroses, Kate Fillion gives the impression that she is simply repeating what Eric and his family have said. The journalist gives way to the admirer with statements such as this:

"Most remarkable, given his on-ice ferocity, are his unforced good manners."[8]

The article does not tell us anything new, merely confirming what everyone has known for a long time. It also makes us more aware than ever of the way the Lindroses take advantage of a journalist they

---

8 Fillion, Kate, "The Next One, eh?" *Chatelaine*, Vol. 64, No. 12, December 1991, p. 79.

trust. Kate Fillion sounds like a friend of the family, or perhaps she just succumbed to the charm of the young hockey star. She tells us that at the end of the interview, Eric gallantly offered, since it was getting dark, to give her a ride home. She doesn't inform us of the highlights of the drive home except that it took place to the sound of the rock band, Journey.

The Lindroses may have a soft spot in their hearts for Kate Fillion, but that is certainly not true of Christie Blatchford, whose article, "What will it be, Eric, hockey or Hollywood?" appeared in the *Financial Post on* November 1, 1991. Blatchford has managed to enter Eric's universe in a way that no one before her has dared to do, and she does not hesitate to say what she sees.

"He is, it seems, fully committed to only one thing, one person — himself."

She then proceeds to evaluate Lindros's decision not to report to the Quebec Nordiques in these words:

"The decision that seemed at once brave and foolish when he made it, is looking increasingly foolish."

As she digs deeper, she realizes just how wrong Eric has been and leaves us in no doubt whatsoever as to her opinion, telling us, "It is time, I think, for Lindros to bite the bullet — to speak for himself; to commit himself to the game that will one day make him rich".

At the moment, Blatchford feels that Eric is acting like a dilettante, and she concludes with a reference to Bonnie who once said her son was so good that perhaps he should be living on another planet. "Well, it already exists," Blatchford remarks. "It's called Hollywood. Eric Lindros is halfway there."

It is easy to imagine the hue and cry that would have followed this highly critical article if it had been written by a Francophone from Quebec. Fortunately, Christie Blatchford is an English-speaking Torontonian. But what audacity, what nerve she has had!

The one article that does justice to Eric as an athlete in purely objective terms is the one written by Leigh Montville in the September 23, 1991 issue of the American magazine, *Sports Illustrated*. The story appeared under the title "Young Gun" and subtitle "Big, rough and only 18, Eric Lindros is poised for NHL stardom, but he wants to achieve it on his terms". Montville focuses on Eric's exceptional talent, which no one has ever doubted. From the American point of view, the problem with the Nordiques is so insignificant that it barely exists. It is not surprising, then, that the article glosses over Eric's refusal to report to the Nordiques. Americans think that everything Lindros says or does is right; he is simply too gifted to be wrong.

In another American magazine, *Inside Sports*, the Lindros story is covered by Stan Fischler, a veteran of the U.S. hockey world and a regular contributor to the Canadian bible, *The Hockey News*. Fischler always has something to say and he says it frankly, honestly and without reservation.

Q. How do our neighbours to the south perceive Eric?

A. My impression, which is shared by a number of my colleagues, is that he is a very arrogant kid.

Q. Do you agree with the stand he has taken with regard to the Nordiques?

A. Not really. Maurice Richard wrote that Eric is going to be another Doug Wickenheiser. I don't totally agree with that, but I have some reservations about his impact.

I should mention that Fischler likes to sew the seeds of controversy and generally expresses an opinion contrary to that of the majority in his attempt to stir things up. But that does not mean he is always wrong. And his colourful language often conveys a very clear message.

Q. What do you think of the Lindroses?

A. We have an expression here in Brooklyn. Do you know where that is?

(Note how an American thinks that we Canadians are all ignoramuses who have never been outside of our little villages.)

Q. Yes, I know where it is. What's your expression?

A. They think their shit does not stink!

He may just be right about that.

On a much more serious and thoughtful note, one of the most distinguished journalists in English Canada, Jeffrey Simpson, parliamentary columnist for *The Globe and Mail* in Ottawa, refers to Eric Lindros in an article about Newfoundland premier, Clyde Wells, another of Quebec's "beloved heros". According to Simpson, "In Quebec, Mr. Wells's abiding opposition to Meech Lake made him as popular as Eric Lindros."

Shortly after I read that appropriate comment, I contacted Simpson, who was quite willing to share his feelings about the Lindros affair with me. He expressed his thoughts in impeccable French.

A. Lindros clearly reflects the opinion of a large segment of the English-speaking population in Canada who don't trust Quebec.

Q. But he's young. Don't you think his generation is more open-minded?

A. He's swallowed all the rumours about the way English-speaking minorities are treated in Quebec. He's only 18 and isn't very sophisticated when it comes to culture or politics.

Let's move on from the serious to the ridiculous. A Quebec magazine called *CROC* is somewhat similar to the English *MAD* magazine, relying on dark humour that is not always in the best of taste. The October issue was devoted to hockey and included some highly questionable, racist pictures and references to Eric Lindros, which were not intended to be taken seriously.

Unfortunately, some people took what they saw in the magazine literally, with results you would expect. John Gardner, president of the Metropolitan Toronto Hockey League, was one of those who took strong exception to the content of the October issue of *CROC*. On October 24, 1991, he used his weekly column in the *The Toronto Star* to express his indignation this way:

"One has to wonder to what extent journalistic freedom should go, especially when it crosses over the obvious boundary line of outright defamation."

To justify his criticism, Gardner compares *CROC* with Don Cherry's performance every Saturday night between the first and second periods of the game on CBC's *Hockey Night in Canada*. However, to justify its excesses, *CROC* hides behind the cover of its black humour that appeals only to a small audience. But Don Cherry uses the most popular of the public media — television — to spread his dangerous, narrow-minded message to an unsuspecting public, who may accept his wild imaginings as the absolute truth.

Gardner feels that Cherry's first show this season was the best of his career. When asked about Lindros on the show, Cherry defended Eric's position in his usual outrageously aggressive style.

"How," retorted Cherry , "can you ask a young Canadian to go to an environment where the majority don't want to be part of this nation, where the language you speak is virtually outlawed (only the signs for now), and to a franchise where even now their top player has no corporate endorsements?"

It would take forever to list all the ludicrous arguments Cherry used in this lamentable broadcast of "Coach's Corner". Suffice it to say that he ends his speech by insulting the Nordiques management, calling them "dumb, dumb, dumb".

Don Cherry is a sad case. What is particularly distressing is that, although everyone considers him to be intolerant, an incorrigible redneck, he is allowed to air his twisted opinions on prime time TV on a regular basis. How can a government-owned corporation justify selling this kind of product? The CBC has washed its hands of the whole thing, saying that the show is a private production of Molstar, but the argument does not stand up, since the network has rights over the content of everything it broadcasts. Productions far less offensive than this one have been treated much more severely by the politicians in Ottawa.

On *La Soirée du Hockey*, the French-language equivalent to "Coach's Corner" is the Mario Tremblay report. Mario Tremblay has his own unique style and is quite popular. He sometimes makes provocative comments in an effort to stir up his viewers, but if he ever tried to express unacceptable, narrow-minded or racist opinions, he would be disciplined immediately, and rightly so.

Don Cherry, on the other hand, makes racist comments on a regular basis. "The Swedes are all a bunch of sissies"; "The Russians are just Communists who only come here to steal Canadians' jobs"; "None of the Europeans have any business in the National Hockey League." I could go on and on. So we shouldn't be surprised that kids from English Canada, who soak up the words of this moron every single week, grow up repeating his idiotic remarks, or that Eric Lindros, despite his exceptional talent, considers Quebec to be hostile territory.

Hockey Night in Canada is guilty all the way down the line. Not only does the show allow Cherry to say what he wants, it actually encourages him to be as outrageous as possible. Why? Because of the ratings. "Coach's Corner" is a goldmine. Journalists flock to the pressrooms during Saturday night hockey games because they don't want to miss Don Cherry. Everyone makes fun of him, nobody takes him seriously, but they all want to watch him, listen to him and criticize him. Cherry makes people laugh—but he is not funny.

Unfortunately, what may seem amusing to an adult who has learned not to take him at face value will have a different effect on a child or teenager who is not yet mature enough to differentiate between the serious and the ridiculous. When Don Cherry points his finger and exclaims "Kyubec, dumb, dumb, dumb", he is expressing an opinion held by many Anglophones like John Gardner, who is president of an organization which is supposed to be developing a new generation of hockey players. Like Eric Lindros, for example.

On Saturday November 16, in a *La Presse* column, Michel Marois describes Cherry in rather explicit terms, calling him "stupid, ridiculous, bigoted, provocative, racist, idiotic, sexist and opinionated". Ron McLean, who is intelligent, cultured and broad minded, has the job of playing opposite to Don Cherry on "Coach's Corner". McLean keeps asking how Cherry can make such outrageous remarks, but he needs to be reminded that the accomplice is just as guilty as the thief. Whether McLean likes it or not, by allowing his name to be linked with Cherry's, he is endorsing the message.

On top of everything else, Cherry is a strong supporter of fighting in hockey. Of course he is. "Mister Macho" cannot conceive of the possibility that a man worthy of being called a man could ever be opposed to violence, although Wayne Gretzky, Mario Lemieux and a number of others have been campaigning to have the NHL eliminate the useless brawls that are now so much a part of hockey. It should come as a surprise to no one that Eric Lindros is on Don Cherry's side in this debate.

I also want to mention an article by Thomas Hurka that appeared in *The Globe and Mail*'s "Fifth Column" and began "What do Eric Lindros and the constitutional debate have in common? More than you think", says Thomas Hurka. Hurka, a philosophy professor at the University of Calgary, suggests that Eric clearly wants to destroy the system. In doing this, he is supporting the philosophical theory of favouring individual over collective rights. Hurka sees a parallel between Eric Lindros's approach and the position of the Reform Party which has been gaining popularity in Western Canada, like the COR in the Maritimes. According to Hurka, "Too often there's an oversimple contrast between individual and collective rights. Rights protect interests, (. . .) but it doesn't follow that the best way to protect interests is by granting only individual rights."

Hurka makes a heroic effort to analyze the policies of the Reform Party, with reference to Senate reform in particular. He concludes with this double message: "If (the party) is really committed to individualism, it should give up on Senate reform. As for Mr. Lindros, he should stop whining and play for Quebec."

I am not at all convinced that Eric would be interested in such intellectual considerations. All Eric cares about is his own immediate future and he is not going to let anything stand in the way of his getting what he wants. He is going to determine the course of events and woe betide those who attempt to obstruct his path. And woe betide those who do not obey his instructions to the letter—as I know from personal experience.

The Canada Cup Tournament gave Eric Lindros the opportunity to prove once and for all that he deserved the reputation he had been gaining since he burst onto the hockey scene. A few days after the competition had reached its exciting finish, the media demanded more and more of Eric and those around him. Television station CBVT in Quebec City asked me to prepare a positive story on the young man to offset the negative image that was becoming more and more fixed in the minds of the people of Quebec. I really liked the idea of taking a new approach that would emphasize Eric's human side and I agreed to take the preliminary steps to produce the short documentary.

Yves Boutin, the producer in Quebec City, wanted me to ask the Lindroses for some pictures of Eric when he was little and, if possible, to interview them at home and give TV viewers an opportunity to get to know and hopefully understand them better. In order to get the things I needed, I decided to phone the Lindros home, hoping to speak to Bonnie. Instead, I got Eric, who was already talking to his agent and asked me if I could be quick.

Q. Eric, I'd like to do a short report about you and your family for the Radio-Canada TV station in Quebec City. Could I meet with you today?

A. No. You'll have to contact the Oshawa Generals. They're coordinating all press requests now.

Q. O.K. In the meantime, I'm going to come take some pictures of your house and your street.

A. What? You can't do that. I don't want you to show our house.

Q. Why not?

A. We've got enough problems as it is.

Q. What does that have to do with showing your house?

A. It's nobody's business where I live, and we don't want anyone to know where we live.

Q. O.K., listen. I promise to go along with what you want. When can I meet with you?

A. Maybe on the weekend. We'll see.

Shortly after I hung up, the cameraman said he was ready and that he did not have much time. We left right away, discussing what we had to do as we drove.

The cameraman was Peter Badcock, a man of about fifty, who had been with the CBC for many years. He is one of the top people in his field and unfailingly conscientious as well. He is not only a true professional who does impeccable work, he is also a gentleman in every sense of the word, who never has anything bad to say about anyone.

I filled him in on the conversation I had just had with Eric and asked his opinion about Eric's request.

A. Well, Daniel, I think we have to respect his wishes.

Q. Then we don't take any pictures of his house?

A. Or at least not to use them on the air.

Q. O.K. Peter. But we're going there anyway. Why don't we take some pictures of the neighbourhood for the archives?

A. What kind of pictures do you want?

Q. To make sure no one can identify the name of the street or the number of the house, take a long shot, just to show what the neighbourhood looks like.

When we got near the Lindroses' street, we chose a corner about a block away from their home, and Peter started filming. We had only been there for a few minutes when Eric, who had noticed Peter and the camera from a distance came charging out of the house, jumped into his Jeep and revved it to the Radio-Canada van. He stopped near the driver's door and yelled at us with menace in his voice, "I can't believe you're doing this."

I answered, "Eric, it's only for archives purposes. I don't intend to use the shot in the story."

Then, without another word, he took off again.

If looks could kill, I wouldn't be here to tell the story.

"That's an angry young man" was Peter's comment.

We finished our work and left for Oshawa. As part of our report, we were going to interview Rick Cornacchia as well as two young Francophones, Jason Campeau and Stéphane Yelle, who had recently joined the Generals. Throughout the drive, we tried to analyze the event we had just witnessed. We agreed that Eric tends to be impulsive, and that we would probably not be able to bring him around to the idea of an interview for Radio-Canada television in the near future. I myself attributed Eric's impatience to the fact that he was tired, almost exhausted from the intense experience of participating in the Canada Cup Tournament.

In Oshawa, we interviewed Eric's two young team-mates and the Generals' coach and then came back to Toronto late in the afternoon. Newsroom editor Michel Racine greeted us with a shout as we entered the Radio-Canada offices. In his usual cynical tone, he hurled this question at me:

Q. Would you like to tell me what you've been doing? The telephone hasn't stopped ringing.

A. What's going on, Michel?

Q. The Radio-Canada lawyers have called. The Chief Editor called from Ottawa, somebody from *The Journal*, and a guy from CBC Network Sports.

A. And just what do all these wonderful people want?

Q. How should I know? It seems the Lindroses are all worked up about something.

This is probably what happened. After Eric drove away, he told his parents and his agent that we had taken pictures of their house without permission. The Lindroses did not wait for so much as a second before they set out to make sure the film would not be used.

Apparently some people in high places had got hold of the story and tried to influence and even threaten the people in the Radio-Canada newsroom, an act that probably did not do much to improve the relationship between the Lindroses and some CBC employees. As a result of the incident, some of the stories in the works at both CBC Sports and the prestigious show, *The Journal*, were also placed in a precarious position. This explained some of the calls Michel Racine had received.

As for the calls from the legal department of Radio-Canada, the lawyers had just spoken to Denis D'Amours, the Chief Editor in Ottawa, to tell him that there was no way anyone could prevent us from broadcasting the kind of pictures Peter and I had taken.

What a mess I was in! Not with the Lindroses but with the newsroom staff, who were pressuring me to use this picture which suddenly became a symbol, not only of the controversy itself, but also of the sacred principle of freedom of expression so dear to the hearts of journalists. No reporters would ever submit to outside influences intended to control the form or content of their work.

After thinking the matter over carefully, I decided to stick to my original plan and not use the picture in question. It simply did not belong in the report I was doing, which, incidentally, was never broadcast.

The story did not end there. When I got home that evening, I noticed that there were a number of messages on my answering machine. Four of them are worth mentioning.

I should explain that my answering machine has all the most recent features. It gives not only the day and time of the calls, but also the telephone number from which the calls were made.

The first call had come from Rick Curran at 4:20 P.M., asking me to call him back in Philadelphia.

The next three calls were all from the same number: 782-4973, the Lindroses' home number.

1) 5:55 P.M. — they hung up
2) 5:56 P.M. — a brief, very aggressive message: "Call Patrick Watson, now!"
3) 5:58 P.M. — "Daniel, I just phoned a minute ago. It's Bonnie Lindros. Carl has phoned Patrick Watson to talk about what happened to our home and our privacy today. We're very, very disappointed . . ."

Patrick Watson is the president of CBC-Radio-Canada. The only person with more clout than he has is Brian Mulroney. The Lindroses had decided to get involved in a very serious game — trying to stop information from being broadcast. At the same time, they hoped to see a negative report filed on a journalist who had dared to go against their wishes — or so they thought.[9]

All their lives the Lindroses have shown a need to have almost total control over their environment, and up to that point, they had almost always succeeded. Now, however, they had come up against a brick wall in the form of the National Hockey League. It was becoming obvious that they would stop at nothing, since they were now trying to control the flow of public information. If you don't bend to their will, watch out!

Reviewing the media reports for this book has made me even more aware of how Eric, Carl and Bonnie Lindros have used their position to dominate everyone around them. They inspire fear because they have power. Several journalists are afraid of them and most Toronto sports journalists do not dare to say anything negative about the Lindros universe. It is easy to understand why. The members of the press need the Lindros clan to provide material for their columns. What is not so easy to understand, however, is why most of them close their eyes to the most obvious facts. One day, they are going to have to admit that, despite his enormous talent and incredible strength, despite his undeniable superiority, Eric Lindros is just another hockey player, and they cannot let an 18-year-old kid control their lives.

Journalists are often criticized because, when they need to protect their own interests or the interests of the people they are reporting on, they occasionally set aside certain principles such as the public's right to be given information. This situation is not exclusive to sports, as you soon discover when you talk to some parliamentary reporters and see how often they are at the mercy of their contacts. For example, journalist James Bennet, who writes for *The Washington Monthly*, calls the White House press corps "The Flak Pack" because it has such a cosy relationship with President Bush.

---

9 After I checked with Nicole Latreille, Patrick Watson's *chef de cabinet*, I learned that Carl Lindros had called the office, but had not been put through to Watson. Carl apparently left several (confused) messages on the office answering machine.

Many sports journalists boast of their friendship with famous professional athletes as if that somehow made them more worthy in the eyes of others. One of my friends in the press gallery at Blue Jays games was really proud of the fact that she had George Bell's private, unlisted telephone number. Apparently she thought this was a great honour!

The most competent and respected journalists are usually those who keep their distance from the people they have to observe or criticize. You have to be skeptical about articles or stories by journalists who maintain very close ties with athletes, artists or politicians.

Any members of the press who claim to be good friends of Eric Lindros are not to be trusted. They are in great danger of thinking like Eric and being at his mercy.

Like his parents, whose example he naturally follows, Eric rebels against everyone who does not share his point of view. He is the product of an education which has made him morbidly afraid of people outside his own world and he may never be able to overcome his fear. To him it is a foregone conclusion that he will not go to live in Quebec City, because anything different, anything that removes him from the comfortable world he has always known represents a threat.

Eric himself has admitted that when he first went to live in Detroit before joining the Oshawa Generals, he was so scared of being alone in a strange place he locked himself in the bathroom.

Eric likes Toronto journalists and is not afraid of them because he knows that they think the way he does. Quebec journalists, on the other hand, are total strangers; therefore, it is entirely natural for him to be frightened of them and for them to find him intimidating. As a consequence, Eric feels ill at ease with the whole province of Quebec, except for a small neighbourhood in Montreal. Here he knows he can be comfortable because he will find a society exactly like the one he has known all his life. As for the United States, clearly that is also a world he would like. At heart, an English Canadian is an American who doesn't know it.

When Eric asked me not to take pictures of the Lindros house, he was issuing an order, and when he gives an order, he expects it to be obeyed. It is a habit he has picked up over the years. Until now, most people have probably complied with his directives, including the journalists who have dealt with him.

The day we took the picture, Eric was acting just like his mother. At times of stress, most of us react the way our role models would, and in that respect, his behaviour was perfectly natural. It is a well-known fact that Bonnie has a tendency to send media people on their way if she doesn't like them, and she is not a good listener. It is therefore quite possible that Eric simply was not paying attention when I said, "I don't intend to use the shot in the story, Eric. It's only for archives purposes."

It is also possible that Eric heard me but did not believe me. That would be too bad, because it is a Lindros family trait to distrust outsiders who, they believe, only want to hurt them.

Throughout this unfortunate adventure, Rick Curran has proved to be no help at all. When I filled him in on the extent of the problem and explained that it would be in the family's best interest to speak to me so that they could say they were sorry and clear the air, Curran just ignored the whole story and said, "I'm not surprised; I know how they operate."

The Lindroses have had all kinds of opportunities to resolve this awkward situation. They have chosen not to act, and probably believe to this day that they have done nothing wrong.

As Paul Lewicki said:

"The Lindroses are only semi-happy when they call most of the shots."

Chapter 5

FROM WAYNE GRETZKY TO ERIC LINDROS

I t was almost mythical.

It was Saturday night at Maple Leaf Gardens in Toronto, November 2, 1991. As usual, the Los Angeles Kings had just swept up the dead, dry Maple Leafs. And, true to form, "The Great One" had been chosen second star of the game, leaving the first star, almost out of politeness, to another fan favourite, Luc Robitaille. In fifteen years in Toronto, I had never seen such a crowd at the dressing room door. The autograph seekers who were there in droves weren't all children, either.

Inside the dressing room, Number 99 was giving a mini press conference as politely as ever, although the journalists' questions were even more insipid and cliché-ridden than usual. Besieged from all sides, Gretzky just kept on smiling, which was perfectly reasonable. Not only had he just turned in an almost unbelievable performance, he had also learned earlier that Walter, his father and best friend, was improving and was going to recover from an aneurism he had suffered a few weeks before.

Suddenly, another star from not so long ago appeared in the doorway of the dressing room: the Golden Jet. Gretzky's smile became a genuinely delighted laugh as the two heros embraced. Wayne and Bobby managed to find a quiet corner — not an easy task in the circumstances — where they could talk quietly, away from the prying eyes and ears of the media.

I watched them for a while from a distance. It was a fantastic sight even for me who, after so many years, had sometimes found the hockey greats less than enthralling.

By the time they had finished talking, the dressing room was beginning to empty. Bobby Hull greeted as many people as he could. When he came up to me, he held out his hand a little mechanically. He probably vaguely remembered my face but couldn't put a name to it. I tried to jog his memory by saying "Bonjour" with a slight English accent, knowing my name was stored somewhere in his brain.

Q. Do you have a minute, Mr. Hull?

A. Give me a second, I'll be right back.

It wasn't the first time I had approached Hull with a microphone. I was a young reporter in Winnipeg when he left the Chicago Black Hawks and, with a bold leap of faith, joined the World Hockey Association. I got to know him a bit and to like him, and I knew that he was always willing to answer journalists' questions no matter what the circumstances.

Q. I'm writing a book about the Lindros affair and I was wondering if you could tell me what you think about this future hockey star.

A. Sure, what would you like to know?

Q. As you probably know, Eric has refused to play for the Quebec Nordiques. Does that surprise you?

A. First of all let me say that I would have played anywhere at his age. I'd even have played in Chibougamau!

This touch of humour was indicative of how very pleasant this great player of the sixties could be. And it was a mark of respect too, since he knew very well that the name of a small town in Quebec would strike a sensitive chord with this interviewer.

Q. Does that mean you don't approve of what he did?

A. Not necessarily. I have mixed feelings about the whole thing. At first, from my 23 years experience in professional hockey, I thought that he should play by the rules. But then I thought, there are so few players of his calibre—Gretzky, Lemieux, Brett Hull— that the League should accommodate them because the game of hockey derives so many benefits from these exceptional athletes. In other words, to ensure that they perform at their best, why not do everything possible to make them happy and productive?

This was surprising coming from Bobby Hull, especially compared to the views of most of the other stars from his era, who are quick to criticize Lindros's decision. Gordie Howe, for example, reacted strongly when I asked him about the situation.

Q. The Québécois can't understand why Eric is refusing to come play for the Nordiques. Can you?

A. You'd have to get inside his mind to find out. I've gone on record as saying—and I've heard Wayne say the same thing—I wish he would have put the sweater on and be whatever it may be. I'd like him to at least give it a try, with the option in the contract where, I don't like you or you don't like me, I'm out of here next year.

The man they call "Mr. Hockey" speaks from the heart when he talks about Eric. There is even a slight note of impatience in his voice when he adds:

A. He's losing a third of the population in Canada if he turns down the French people. They've always treated the Howe family so good.

Even Bobby Orr, whose father the Lindroses had gone to for advice a few years ago, has some reservations about Eric. When I told him what people in Quebec think about Eric refusing to play for the Nordiques, that they didn't really understand it, he just said:

A. Nor do I!

A short answer but very eloquent! If the Gordie Howe and Bobby Orr can't solve the Lindros mystery, who can?

When asked what they think of this "fat cat" era which allows the most talented players to show their independence, most former players just say "times have changed". Eric Lindros is not the first to have expressed a preference, indicating that he would not play for certain teams. Twice in the last ten years, warnings have been issued to the Toronto Maple Leafs by potential candidates in the universal draft. Craig Redmond and Craig Simpson both let the Leafs know that they were not interested in a career in Toronto. Simpson had informed the Maple Leaf management in writing that he would not report to the team if he was drafted in his first year of eligibility. The Leafs took Wendel Clark over him that year and Simpson went to Pittsburgh. Simpson now plays for Edmonton since the trade which sent Paul Coffey to the Penguins.

Simpson is not the most talkative of players, a trait which was clear when I talked to him about being drafted by the Leafs. But he did confirm that it was all true and that his decision was made long before the 1985 June draft. The Leafs have never denied the story but they insist that Simpson was never part of their plans anyway. Simpson says that the main reason he didn't want to play for the Leafs had nothing to do with the city or the money. He was just not impressed by the quality of the organization. What would he have done if the Leafs had ignored his request? Simpson would have gone back to school and continued playing in the United States—a logical answer for someone who had chosen to play college hockey rather than junior hockey.

The most interesting case of a dispute with the draft system is the case of Jeff Greenlaw who was the Washington Capitals' first choice in 1986. Although he was only 16 years old, Greenlaw had been chosen by the North Bay Centennials of the OHL. Jeff was not too happy about the situation; so he took a chance and challenged the league's draft system in court. He lost the case and finally opted to play American college hockey.

The Lindros clan certainly took this case into consideration when they decided not to challenge either the Ontario or the NHL draft. Instead they just sulked in their corner and pressured the teams involved to bow to their demands.

* * *

Opinions expressed by hockey players about other players rarely break certain rules of etiquette. A John Kordic or a Bob Probert may fight it out on the ice but you never hear them criticize each other after the game. At worst, the player who lost the fight will say something like: "I'll get him next time" or "He had an unfair advantage in the circumstances".

But Eric Lindros doesn't always play by these rules of decency. In his autobiography, he talks about Dave Chyzowski and a vicious check he took, one Eric says he won't forget. You don't invite Dave and Eric to the same party unless you want to see a good fight. They just can't stand each other! Chyzowski doesn't deny that Lindros is not one of his favourites.

Q. Why?

A. I think the trouble between us started when we were trying out for the world junior team a couple of years back. It was in the summer of 1989 at the first tryout camp and I didn't know who he was. He was just sixteen and I had just been drafted that year and I guess I was one of the bigger guys and so was he. Then after we both made the team, we went to Finland. I was doing well and scored a few goals but he didn't have a great tournament. He tried to blame the other guys and the way the tournament was set up. His mother was complaining about who he was playing with and going to the coach.

Q. What was your reaction then?

A. Who was I to say anything? He felt he should have been the best player and he wasn't.

Q. Is that all?

A. No. When we (the Kamloops Blazers) went to the Memorial Cup, he was yapping all the time. I gave him a crosscheck into the boards and he complained about it. Someone said his mother wanted to sue me.

Q. Do you hold it against Eric?

A. I've got nothing against him and I'm not out to get him or anything. I've seen some of the things he has done that blow my mind.

Q. What do you think of him?

A. He can be really cocky. I mean, you've got to be cocky to be a hockey player, but when I first met him I asked him a couple of questions and he just told me how good he was and what he wanted to do with his life.

Q. He mentions you in his book; he hasn't forgotten what you did to him.

A. If he's out to get me, so be it. I can't spend my life worrying about Eric Lindros. Things do go on in the heat of the battle, but it's not fair to say anything discriminatory against anyone. If I had been drafted by Quebec, I would have gone there. It's every kid's dream to be in the NHL. The way Eric Lindros has been doing it is a little selfish. You can't think you're better than the league. I think it's unfortunate he's not playing because he has got a tremendous amount of talent. What it's coming down to is he doesn't want to go to a French community.

If Eric Lindros is anxious to meet up with Dave Chyzowski again, there are also people who can't wait for Lindros to play in the NHL. Gino Odjik for example.

The Odjik case raises a sensitive and serious issue. Odjik is a young man with limited potential for a career in hockey. Drafted 86th in the 1990 draft by the Vancouver Canucks, it is highly likely that Odjik will have to settle for a secondary role with an NHL team throughout his career, because his talent is limited according to observers. There is a place for him, but he will clearly never be a great star. However, that didn't stop Gino Odjik from indicating publicly, by both word and deed, that he has a profound dislike for Eric Lindros. Gino refused to shake Eric's hand at the end of an exhibition game between the Vancouver Canucks and Team Canada as is the custom in Olympic competition. He explained why to reporters in the dressing room right after the game. I met Gino when the Canucks were in Toronto in December and asked him about the incident with Eric Lindros.

Q. What don't you like about Lindros?

A. He doesn't like the French; I don't understand why.

Q. What exactly did he do to you?

A. It's not what he did, it's what he said.

Q. What was that?

A. He insulted me during the Memorial Cup two years ago. He called me a "goddamn frog" and "goddamn Indian".

Q. But surely he isn't the only hockey player who does that sort of thing?

A. No, that's true. But he does it for no reason, without provocation, even before the game.

Q. Why did you wait so long before coming out with this in public?

A. Two years ago, the situation wasn't as serious. Now that he's said he won't play for Quebec, he's insulted all Quebeckers. I come from Quebec and I'm proud of it.

Odjik's accusations added fuel to the flames which had been ignited a few months earlier by other similar comments made by Martin Lapointe of the Detroit Red Wings. When I talked to Martin about it in September, he seemed so embarrassed that his face turned as red as his sweater.

Q. You really started something by making those accusations against Eric. Do you take back what you said about him calling you a "bloody frog"?

A. No. What I said is true. But let's not exaggerate. It's not the end of the world.

Martin and Eric had a chance to talk it over later when the Oshawa Generals were in Detroit. Martin then said that everything had been forgotten.

Q. You didn't really mean what you said?

A. It's not that. It's just that Eric and I talked it over. There are no hard feelings. It's history. It's over.

Martin doesn't want to talk about it. Unfortunately for him, the fire has not been extinguished so easily, especially because some other players, including Pierre Sévigny and Patrice Brisebois, witnessed the incident. Sévigny, the live wire of the group, describes what he saw:

A. The incident involving Martin did happen.

Q. What about you? Did you get along well with Eric?

A. We were always teasing each other; it didn't mean anything.

As for Patrice Brisebois he is more inclined to praise Eric.

Q. What do you think of him?

A. Eric is arrogant; it's understandable. He's always been the best.

Q. What kind of relationship did you have with him?

A. I did my own thing, he did his. He didn't talk to me, I didn't talk to him.

Q. Does it bother you that he doesn't want to play in Quebec?

A. If he has any pride at all and if he really thinks he can carry a team on his shoulders, he should do it with the Nordiques. He should at least try!

Alain Vigneault, one of the coaches with the Canadian junior team, tries to sweeten the pill in discussing Eric's relationship with his Francophone team-mates.

A. Maybe there was some friction in the dressing room, but they were minor incidents. Otherwise the coaches would have stepped in.

The obvious question is whether Eric Lindros was being racist when he called some of his opponents and team-mates "frog" or "Indian". It's easy to call him racist, but maybe we have to stop and think about the answer first.

A person who is racist looks down on an individual because that individual is a member of a particular group. The group may be defined by any one of a variety of criteria. Language is certainly one of those criteria, cultural or genetic heritage is another. But the crucial term in the definition of racism is the verb "to look down on". If a player insults an opponent by using offensive language, is that an indication that he despises him? Calling someone names, if those names are taken literally, may be a form of basic racism. But if you go beyond the superficial level, you have to ask why it was that one individual insulted the other in the given circumstances. When I'm driving my car and I'm frustrated by a driver who I think is driving too slowly and who happens to be Oriental, I might yell, "Get out of my way, you yellow creep!" Does that mean I'm racist? Or am I just angry because this person who is different from me is preventing me from getting where I want to go and the first thing I see when I look at him is that he is different?

When a hockey player provokes an opponent verbally, either in the heat of the action or later when he gets within hearing distance, he doesn't really mean that he hates him. He's just angry because the other player did something that interfered with his productivity, his performance. The insult is really meant as a display of superior strength and destructive power. Besides, as a general rule, if the person who is insulted in such circumstances is as strong as or even stronger than the other, he will react in one of two ways. If he is really hurt by the insult, he will go out and play even harder to improve his performance and prove his superiority, or he will reply verbally in kind.

Professional athletes who play contact sports are not necessarily being racist when they come out with crude insults. It's just part of the power trip in their competitive world.

This does not mean that racism does not exist in sports. Examples of racism abound. When Conn Smythe (not the trophy but the person it was named after!) spoke in public, he often prefaced his remarks as follows: "Ladies and gentlemen . . . and French-Canadians!" It was an insult to end all insults, a type of humour which barely conceals profound feelings of racial superiority. Smythe was also often overtly racist. He would say to whoever would listen, always supposedly as a joke, that he would give fifteen thousand dollars to anyone who could whitewash Herb Carnegie.[10]

Don Cherry is another one who is unacceptably contemptuous when he goes on and on about the Swedes being just a bunch of sissies.

When an NHL general manager says that a journalist for the *Los Angeles Times* is "not only a fucking nigger, he's also a fucking faggot", that is a good, basic example of racism.

Eric Lindros is no more racist than you or I, no more no less. We can leave him alone on that one.

But it certainly isn't a very dignified tactic for him to use to dominate his opponents, something he should be able to do with just his exceptional talent. There's no reason for him to stoop so low.

In fact, from the way he behaves towards the other hockey players on the ice, on both his team and the opposing team, Eric Lindros shows that he has a very high opinion of himself as a hockey player. He also shows no respect for the other hockey people around him. He wants to be king, he wants to reign supreme. It would be easy to say he suffers from a superiority complex but that isn't quite the right

---

10   Herb Carnegie was a professional hockey player who never made it to the NHL. He played in the now defunct Quebec Senior League. Carnegie was black.

expression in this case, because of course he really is superior to the average player.

Lindros does not find it easy to share his space. That is why he will even go so far as to attack his own team-mates. Jarrold Skalde, a promising player with a great future on the New Jersey Devils, spent more than three seasons in Oshawa. He was finally traded to the Belleville Bulls at his own request. It was no coincidence that the trade came shortly after Eric Lindros arrived in Oshawa.

Q. Did you get along well with Eric?

A. We got along away from hockey. We did things like go out and eat together. But when it came to hockey there was a little bit of a conflict.

Q. What kind of conflict?

A. That first year when he came, it wasn't so bad, but I knew the next year was going to be tough. It was obvious he was going to get all the ice time so I asked to be traded.

Q. What do you think of him now?

A. As a player I really respect him and as a person he's a good guy. It had to be tough for him to concentrate with all that media attention.

Skalde is quite prepared to say what he thinks about Eric's attitude to the Nordiques. He admits that he has mixed feelings about the stand Eric has taken. Although he thinks it took courage for Eric to support free choice for hockey players, he still can't see why he won't go to Quebec.

A. I'm kind of split about what he's doing. It's good for him that he's saying hockey players should be able to decide where they live. It's about time somebody makes the point that we should have some say. On the other hand, it has given him a bad image. A lot of players call him a suck. A lot of that is jealousy. The year we won the Memorial Cup there wasn't much talk about him going to Quebec, but the year I got traded, the guys were all over him about going to Quebec and I think that really got to him.

Eric Lindros leaves a pretty strong impression on most of the people he has played with, even briefly. Rob Cimetta, for example, was born in Toronto and played junior hockey in Toronto. He was drafted by the Boston Bruins and then came back to Toronto after being traded for Steve Bancroft. Cimetta knew Eric when he was only sixteen years old and both of them had been invited to the national junior team camp.

Q. You're from Toronto like Eric and you know him. Are you surprised by what he has said?

A. He's using the old financial reasons not to go to Quebec. If he's after money, Quebec offered him a lot. I don't agree with what he is doing. I think it should be an honour to be the first pick over all and he should at least give that city a chance; I'm sure they would welcome him with open arms.

Cimetta is not the only one who thinks so. But there aren't many players of Eric's generation and background who have the courage to say so in such definite terms.

Two young players already in the NHL, Pierre Turgeon and Benoît Hogue, come from very different backgrounds than Eric. They both came from Quebec and went first to Buffalo and then to New York. They had to cope with a completely new environment, learn a new language and adapt to a very different lifestyle from the one they were used to. Pierre found it difficult at first, especially because both the public and the media had very high expectations of him. He was supposed to fill the skates of Gilbert Perreault, the best player in Buffalo history, and he was expected to make the Sabres a winning team.

Q. What do you think about Eric Lindros' problems?

A. I don't think he really knows Quebec City. If he went there, he would have an opportunity to learn a new language like I did when I arrived in Buffalo. Now I'm glad I learned English. I think he'd already made up his mind about Quebec without even trying to give it a chance. Its a super city with terrific fans. He doesn't know what he's missing.

Benoît Hogue is in complete agreement with his friend, adding:

A. If he's so great, this is the perfect chance to prove it. First of all he could help the Nordiques win the Stanley Cup; then he could prove that he can adapt to another environment. If I can leave my city, my province, my country to pursue my career elsewhere, he should be able to do it too. It sure wasn't easy at first, but now everything's O.K.

Benoît ranks high on my list of quality hockey players. He's not a superstar, quite the contrary. According to an annual assessment by a group of pseudo-expert Toronto analysts, he is only a marginal player. Two years ago, Benoît was ranked dead last in a comparative study of all active players in the NHL. I mentioned this to him during one of our meetings and that triggered a smile. In fact, the reason why I think so highly of Benoît is that he holds his head up and he's proud of his background and his opinions. Last year in Buffalo, Benoît came to blows with one of his team-mates, Dean Kennedy, during a Sabres' practice because he was fed up with Kennedy calling him a frog.

Q. He really got to you, as they say.

A. Yes. In the heat of the moment, during a game, lots of things happen. You often get called names. But during a practice, by a guy whose supposed to be on your side, I couldn't take it.

Q. What happened after that?

A. Well, it didn't happen again, and I also think the players felt closer to each other afterwards.

Q. Eric Lindros has a reputation for teasing French-speaking players like that. Does that bother you?

A. Sure it bothers me when I hear it, but I think he's just a little immature.

Of all the players who knew Eric Lindros well during the famous junior championships in Finland, Steven Rice impresses me the most. Steven is now playing for the Edmonton Oilers, after being acquired in the famous trade which sent Mark Messier to the New York Rangers. I spoke with Steven after a long Oilers practice at Maple Leaf Gardens.

Q. You knew him really well. What do you think of him?

A. You almost have to feel sorry for him — to be eighteen years old and to have to live like an adult! He's still a kid and he just wants to have fun. You don't want to be eighteen and miserable.

Q. And does his refusal to negotiate with Quebec surprise you?

A. No. They've already changed rules for him, one in the OHL —
    being able to trade your first round pick. And now in the NHL—
    he can come back any time. They're giving him all the opportu-
    nity to play in the league. He could be a star in this league right
    now.

Q. But he's a pretty good hockey player, right?

A. Sure, but the thing is, Mario Lemieux, Wayne Gretzky, nobody
    is better than the game. He plays the game, he's not better than
    the game. Look at Gretzky. He's one of the most modest guys
    you'll ever meet; he's broken every record you could ever set for
    a centerman in the NHL. Gretzky is the classiest guy you'll ever
    want to meet and he always takes care of the people that have
    helped him. . . . Eric is only eighteen; he hasn't had a chance to
    do that yet, but . . . if he doesn't, that's a big loss for Eric.

Wayne Gretzky has often been asked what he thinks of Eric Lindros.
It doesn't seem to bother him that Lindros is featured in the media
everywhere. He simply says that, yes, Lindros is in a class by himself
as far as talent and potential is concerned. But if you listen carefully
to what Wayne says, there is often a hidden meaning in his words,
a subtle message for Eric.

A. He's eighteen and at that age, everybody thinks they know
    what's best. By the time you realize what your father was telling
    you was true, your own kids are telling you you're wrong.

There are many parallels between Gretzky and Lindros. They are
both blessed with exceptional natural talent and there are similarities
in the way their careers have developed. Like Lindros, Gretzky was
drafted by Sault Ste. Marie of the OHL. And just like the Lindros
family, the Gretzkys were not at all keen on the idea of their son going
to a place 800 kilometres away. But, unlike the Lindroses, the Gretzkys, to their credit, took a second look and changed their minds after
visiting the small northern Ontario town. Wayne finally agreed to
report to the Greyhounds.

In his own way, Wayne Gretzky also challenged the NHL system.
Being too young for the NHL, he got around the problem by starting
his career with the rival World Hockey Association. When it came

time to move on to the big league, he agreed to sell his services to a team in a small centre even though he knew his marketing value would be greater in a big American city. The rest is history; with Gretzky, the Edmonton Oilers went on to win four Stanley Cups.

Eric Lindros faces the same dilemma. However, his reaction is different from Gretzky's and he simply will not rise to the challenge. Walter Gretzky, Wayne's father, has played a dominant role in the important decisions made by his son; Carl Lindros seems to want to play the same role for his son. But the advice offered by the Lindros family is based on a very different set of principles. Although the Gretzkys took their son's interests into account, they did not ignore the established standards and would never have refused to negotiate just to impose their views. Carl and Eric Lindros, on the other hand, refuse to consider any solution other than the one they have chosen. Their way of negotiating is to put a series of options that they consider acceptable on the table. Nothing else interests them.

Q. Wayne, should the league yield to the pressure from the Lindroses?

A. The league needs all the good players available; but it will survive even if some of them don't want to play by the rules.

It's easy, in such a situation, to tell the Quebec Nordiques to forget Eric and trade him as soon as they can because they will never get the Lindroses to change their minds.

Except that that would amount to abdication, pure and simple, which would open the door to a whole new era of challenges. The NHL teams located in small centres would be constantly blackmailed by the best of the players to come. If the Nordiques don't call the Lindros clan's bluff, the whole league will be the loser. And so will the hockey fans because they too will be at the mercy of the whims of every superstar.

Besides, as Wayne Gretzky said:

A. Nobody right now could take the place of an Eric Lindros. No trade would bring this situation to a satisfactory conclusion.

Not even for Wayne Gretzky.

Chapter 6

Marcel Aubut and Pierre Pagé

I first met Marcel Aubut in the early 1980s, when the Nordiques were considered respectable compared to the Maple Leafs, who were then at the height of the Ballard era, or in other words, at the bottom of the standings.

There was no special reason for our meeting. He was passing through Toronto and, since Radio-Canada generally likes to go all the way when a Francophone guest might be available for an interview, I showed up to see him with a TV crew in tow. Aubut was kind enough to agree to an interview then and there.

While Marcel and I waited for the sound and video technicians to finish their interminable tests, we chatted about one thing and another. Since I knew that he had been a good friend of my sister's, I identified myself as Marie's younger brother. After that I could sense that the ice had been broken between us, and our conversation quickly took on a friendly, more light-hearted tone.

Q. Tell me Daniel, how long have you been living in Toronto?

A. Oh, about seven or eight years, I think.

Q. Seven or eight years of the Maple Leafs — you must really be a glutton for punishment! Haven't you had enough yet?

A. Not really. Ballard is a little like Aubut — at least he's never boring!

These last remarks had us both laughing out loud, and I could see that Marcel Aubut was a very warm person with an innate ability to communicate. After all, we knew each other only through third parties, yet here we were establishing contact in the most natural way, with a sense of trust already developing between us.

Our encounters over the course of the following years were always cordial and marked by mutual respect. So it was natural that, where the Lindros story was concerned, Marcel Aubut trusted me.

In September 1991, Eric was in Quebec City with Team Canada. On the Sunday evening before the historic game against the Soviets at Le Colisée, Aubut and I happened to be dining at the same restaurant, Chez Nicola on rue Maguire in Sillery. My sister Marie had passed away during the summer and this was the first time I had seen Marcel since the funeral. It was a rather sad occasion. We began our conversation by exchanging a few words of heartfelt sympathy. Inevitably, we got around to Eric Lindros, and it suddenly dawned on me that the owner of the Nordiques was genuinely upset, despite the impression he always gives of being on top of everything.

Q. Daniel, you must know the Lindroses pretty well by now. Can you tell me anything nice about them?

A. Nothing you don't already know, Marcel. They are one of the most united families in the world.

Q. What about Bonnie? Is she as bizarre as people say?

A. I don't really know. I think her bark is probably worse than her bite.

At the time of the above conversation, I didn't know a tenth of what I now know about the clan, so I had no reason to say anything untoward about what appeared to be a perfectly normal family. Moreover, I sincerely believed that Bonnie Lindros was just another overprotective mother who adored her son.

Had Aubut asked me that question three months later, I would have reacted quite differently. However, it never came up when Marcel and I talked in mid-December, in an interview in which he agreed to answer questions that were much more probing than those that had been asked in Sillery.

Q. Tell me Marcel, do you know how violent a dislike Bonnie Lindros has taken to you?

A. Yes, I've heard all about it.

Q. What did you ever do to make her feel that way?

A. Not a thing.

Q. So how do you explain it?

A. It's simple, Daniel. I'm the one holding the key. That's it in a nutshell. She doesn't even know me. In fact, I've only seen her once.

Q. Only once?

A. That's right. There were a lot of people around. Her husband was there, and so was John Ziegler.

Marcel Aubut showed no sign of losing his temper as he talked. He spoke in a resigned tone, and he sounded a bit sad, perhaps a little impatient, but not at all angry or belligerent.

A. She dislikes anyone who doesn't agree with her, but I happen to be the guy with the key. I'm the one who can say "O.K., I'll trade him", but I don't. That's why she doesn't like me. It can't be anything else.

I was about to ask another question, but Aubut continued talking.

A. She also thinks that I have a lot of influence with the League, because she knows I've accomplished some big things in the past, and that scares her. I think she's convinced herself that I'm planning a coup against her son, that I'm going to get the two years extended to four years . . .

Aubut's comment here about extending the two years to four is a crucial point. The Nordiques do not hold much of a hand, and this may be the last card they have left to play.

The Nordiques have exclusive negotiating rights with Eric Lindros for a period of two years as of the moment they drafted him. If Aubut manages to bring the NHL management around to his point of view, the League could change its rule and extend the ownership period to four years. When I asked John Ziegler, president of the National Hockey League, about that possibility, he thought for a few minutes before giving this rather long answer.

A. Those are items that really don't relate to Mr. Lindros; they relate to issues that we continually have in our collective bargaining discussions. For some time, and long before Mr. Lindros was on the scene, there have been concerns by the general managers, because we're obliged to draft at eighteen, that two years really doesn't provide time for a true look at how a player is going to develop and they would like to have a longer opportunity. So, in that context, this is something that we have in discussion at the collective bargaining level for a few years and will continue to discuss with our counterparts.

John Ziegler takes the time to weigh every word when he gives an opinion on hockey-related issues. If you read his statement carefully, you can see that it is possible to anticipate the kind of change in League policy that Aubut was referring to, provided of course that the Players' Association agrees to it.

You can tell right off when you talk to Ziegler, whether on the telephone or in person, that he does not like to commit himself. Nevertheless, he is willing to answer questions if they are clearly and courteously presented, even if they seem critical of him.

Q. Mr. Ziegler, there are some observers, a good number in fact, who are very disappointed at your apparent inaction in this matter, which has allowed the parties to be pitted against each other. On one side is the best prospect to appear on the hockey scene since Gretzky and Lemieux, and on the other is one of the weakest links in your chain, due to the small size of its market. What do you say in answer to these critics?

A. I think that the critics don't understand either the business or the rights and obligations relating to the situation . . .

Q. In simple terms, what are those obligations?

A. The way the business is conducted, it is the responsibility and the right of each team, with respect to its draft selections, to do as it deems best for its interests. And it would be totally out of place and inappropriate for anybody involved in the League to go assist one team to help improve its competitive position.

What Mr. Ziegler can do, though, is what he has done elsewhere — he can act as a mediator between the two parties. Obviously, he cannot help having the interests of his product at heart. On the other hand, his product depends on the well-being of its members. And since the members include players as well as owners, he would want to please both the Lindros clan and the Nordiques. Therefore, despite an apparent conflict of interest, Ziegler could perform the role of mediator in this case in an honest and satisfactory manner.

Aubut and the Nordiques would be quick to accept such an intervention, although Eric and the rest of the clan would probably, understandably enough, have some qualms, given their position and their extreme distrust of anything that concerns the Quebec Nordiques.

What Ziegler does not want to do if he can help it, is to go for the quick fix. If he does that, it would just cause everyone to lose out. And Marcel Aubut knows it.

A. I'm a lawyer, Daniel, and I understand it all. I don't want Ziegler to intervene, because if he does, he'll harm my case. I'd prefer to work quietly, behind the scenes, with a well-defined strategy, because in the end that's what will get results.

Nordiques management claims that this strategy will produce positive results, but has not disclosed any of its elements. Aubut says that he will achieve his aims. His optimism is obviously shared by his associates, in particular the men who run the team, Pierre Pagé, the general manager, and Gilles Léger, Pagé's assistant.

A. I don't know if Eric is aware of it, but there is a lot we can offer him. He thought at first that we would trade him, but now he realizes that we won't let him go at any price. Not because we wish him any harm, but because we'd like to see him grow with a young team, one which is really starting to come into its own . . .

Gilles Léger is a Franco-Ontarian from Cornwall. His French is typical of that area of the province, with the odd English word thrown in here and there. His thoughts and feelings reflect a mentality peculiar to French-speaking minorities outside Quebec.

A. . . . and will do him a lot of good—he would enjoy the experience and he would have the chance to develop his skills alongside guys his own age who are top notch hockey players. I think it would be good for him, good for the NHL and probably good for the country too.

The notion of mutual respect often comes up when representatives of the Nordiques organization talk about the Lindros clan. I have never heard them say anything, in any of our conversations, that was uncalled for with regard to the clan.

Q. What is your reaction to the position taken by the Lindroses?

A. We have to respect their position, and they have to respect ours. That's the only way we can make any progress. If we don't respect each other, we'll never get anywhere. But respect isn't something you automatically give or get — it has to be earned. I notice that Eric has worked very hard to gain everyone's respect. If he accepts the fact that our goal is to see him prosper along with the team, then I think we will manage to reach an agreement one of these days.

That thought — that one of these days they will manage to reach an agreement — is the driving force behind the strategy of the Nordiques hockey club. Never mind that the signals sent by the Lindros clan do not hold out the slightest ray of hope. These men still believe that Eric Lindros will change his mind about playing for the Nordiques.

Q. What are the odds that you'll get Eric?

A. At this point in time?

Q. Yes, one week before Christmas, 1991.

A. I would say 50-50.

Q. Do you think it's likely to change soon?

A. I think it will go up to 80% after the Olympics and 100% by October 2, 1992.

Marcel Aubut answers the same question with just as much enthusiasm and conviction.

A. I would say there's a 75% chance of success.

Q. Is that the highest you'll go?

A. It's been around that level from the beginning.

Some people think those figures sound like an impossible dream, but Aubut and Léger will tell you that their dream will come true some day. There is no way to persuade them otherwise. Marcel Aubut sees Eric Lindros as the most ambitious project of his career.

Q. Are you really serious when you say that?

A. Absolutely — 75%.

Q. I'm trying my best not to laugh, Marcel. Everybody else says just the opposite.

A. Then you're in for a surprise.

Q. And if, by some miracle, you do succeed, do you think people will forget all the things that have been said?

A. All we need is one game. Just one game with Lindros scoring one or two goals in his blue sweater. They'll all be delirious with joy!

Q. Everything will be forgotten?

A. Everything. Instantly. I know the people of Quebec like the back of my hand!

The delirium Aubut mentioned is a phenomenon the people of Quebec are used to, but you won't find it anywhere else in Canada. Eric Lindros can't begin to imagine what the adulation of a nation can be like. In Quebec, when the crowd cheers a Guy Lafleur, at the Forum or Le Colisée, or a mob forms around a hero, something unique happens, a special intensity fills the air, becoming so palpable you can almost reach out and touch it.

When people applaud their leader with tears streaming down their faces, as they did for René Lévesque at Centre Paul-Sauvé, they don't feel embarrassed or ask themselves why they are crying or worry about how it looks. That kind of emotion simply does not exist in Toronto. It is unlikely that Eric Lindros has ever witnessed a demonstration of that nature or that he would know how to react if he were actually the object of such an emotional outpouring. Indeed, there is some suggestion that he finds the prospect a little frightening. He knows he would get a hero's welcome at Le Colisée. He saw the kind of wild, spontaneous, ear-splitting cheers that greeted Guy Lafleur on the night of the famous game between the USSR and Team Canada. You would never see an ovation like that at Maple Leaf Gardens.

Dave Chambers, head coach of the Nordiques until Pierre Pagé decided to replace him last November, understands perfectly well the message the Lindroses have sent. He lives in Toronto, as they do, and had to assess the Quebec option, as they did. Unlike them, however, he saw it as a challenge.

Q. Do you think Eric would have liked Quebec and the Nordiques?

A. I think he would have been liked. I think he would have been a big hero there, a hero of immense proportions. He would have owned the place. He would have liked it. It's just something he doesn't want to take a chance on.

Q. Do you have any idea why?

A. He only worries about the negatives, which may never happen.

Q. What positive arguments could be given to him?

A. All I know is, if the Nordiques are winning and he's the big player on the team, he would get all the endorsements in Quebec and certainly all the endorsements elsewhere as well.

Dave Chambers was anxious to add that he had met Eric Lindros the previous summer at Collingwood, during the Team Canada training camp. They had spent a few minutes together talking about the Quebec issue.

Q. What did he say at that time?

A. He made it very clear to me that he was not coming and I believed him, right from the start. And I don't think it's just a matter of money. He just believes he doesn't want to go there.

Q. Did you try to sell him on the Nordiques?

A. Oh yes! But it was very clear to me from that conversation that it was not a money issue. It didn't matter how much money they threw at him, he was not coming.

Pierre Pagé is another member of the Nordiques organization who, like Aubut and Léger, refuses to give up and keeps on believing that Eric's categorical no will one day be transformed into an unequivocal yes. One December evening, the day after the Nordiques had suffered another defeat on the road — 3 to 1 in Washington — we had a long talk, and I asked him point blank whether he thought there was still a reasonable chance that Eric would join the Nordiques hockey team.

A. I don't see why not. I don't see any problem, except for those that have been made up where none exist. An athlete, like an artist, is an entertainer. He's supposed to help people relax, smile and forget their troubles. Eric Lindros wants to do that, and he wants to do it soon, with a winning team.

Q. Exactly, Pierre. Just yesterday Eric said, "I want to play with a winner", obviously implying that the Nordiques don't fill the bill. He is right to some extent, don't you think?

A. He says all sorts of things that aren't always based on solid fact. It's easy to say "The Nordiques are losers", but how many players can predict which three or four teams will be at the top in the coming years? Today's players are discussed and debated as never before. Joe Sakic said that we should trade Lindros, yet the day he made that statement we won 7 to 3. Young people will say anything that pops into their heads, so why worry about it— just because they say something doesn't mean that they're right.

It would be nice to be able to share Pagé's optimism, to believe, as he does, that the situation will turn around, but it is hard for most of us to envision that a Lindros would retract statements that have been so inflexible. It seems the Nordiques are still naive and gullible enough to think that this story will have a happy ending.

Q. What means do you have left to bring the story to a successful conclusion?

A. This is a problem that should be resolved with the help of the National Hockey League, because several other teams are going to be affected by similar problems in the coming years. Everyone is laughing at Quebec right now, today it's our turn, but the other teams are going to encounter the same stumbling block at one time or another in the future. We ought to benefit from the experience of other professional leagues. In football and baseball, player contracts must be signed within a very short period of time, whereas in basketball, there are no time restrictions. All that the Nordiques have to do right now is to stay calm, maintain a positive attitude and show that the matter can be negotiated in good faith, thereby demonstrating, in the long run, that living in Quebec City can be a very good experience.

By comparing hockey to basketball, Pagé strengthens his argument, but the comparison with baseball does not help him at all. In baseball, you only have one year to sign a player you have drafted. I pointed this out to Pagé.

A. The NHL is not baseball. We don't have the 24 to 28 million dollars a team that television guarantees to baseball before the doors are even opened.

The more you listen to Pierre Pagé, the better you understand how he manages to maintain both his enthusiasm and his absolute conviction that this complicated situation will turn out well. He simply keeps telling himself that it is only a matter of time until Eric outgrows what appears to be a persecution complex.

A. An athlete is an artist, not a politician. He must accept the fact that it is his job to help take people's minds off their problems.

Before he can do that, he has to settle his own. Eric's biggest problem originates at home. His very strong attachment to his family is becoming increasingly harmful.

Q. You spoke earlier about Eric's relationship with his family, and I hear it caused quite a commotion within the family.

A. All I said was, that if I were Eric's brother, I would remind him that I loved Mom and Dad as much as he did, but that it was about time he started listening to some other, more impartial voices. I know his mother didn't like that, but I was just trying to say what I honestly believed. In real life, parents are not always right about everything. They too need to hear views from neutral sources, to help them see issues more clearly.

One of the obstacles to negotiating with the Lindros clan is that it is almost impossible to speak to Eric on a one-to-one basis. Pierre Pagé has had only one private conversation with Eric, and then it was brief and superficial and lasted about ten minutes.

Q. How did that little conversation go?

A. He started off by telling me straight out that he did not want to come to Quebec.

Q. What was his attitude towards you?

A. Very polite. He is an articulate, intelligent guy, much like his parents actually. They see themselves as pioneers with a mission.

Clearly, Pagé, Léger and Aubut share the same views. All three believe that the rather sharp statements Eric has been making since September are part of the Lindros clan's strategy, in the manner of negotiations between big companies and large-scale unions, in which statements are often made by one side to provoke the other side into taking a more favourable position. Pagé believes that everything Eric has said has been said for the same purpose — to make the other side give in to his demands.

A. I think everybody takes what he says too seriously. I have been travelling outside Quebec for more than twenty years, and I can tell you that there are thousands upon thousands of people who share Eric Lindros's opinions about Quebec. So why should we be surprised by what he says? There are tons of people in Canada and the United States who would never want to live in Quebec, although they don't know much about it, and what they do know is often false, based on bits and pieces of unrelated or negative information. So I am not all that surprised at what Eric and his parents have been saying. However, since their perceptions are not based on fact, we can change the way they see us. One way to do that is to stop being so shocked. We may love our city dearly, but we know very well that there are plenty of people who do not care for the province of Quebec. It is up to us to show them that they are wrong, and to keep our cool while we are at it.

I cannot help but admire the composure demonstrated by these three men who head up the Nordiques organization. In talking about this whole highly emotional story, they have never once lost their patience. Their self-control is all the more impressive because it would have been so easy for them to panic and let themselves be unduly pressured by outside forces into making a trade.

A. Surely comments by the public and the press have affected you at least a little?

A. Everyone is looking for short-term answers, but you can't solve the problem that way. To succeed you must be patient. You try so hard to negotiate in good faith that you risk looking naive. It would be easy to be shocked. I want to tell the people of Quebec that we have to change our perceptions too. We may not want to try. It's harder than you think, but it's worth it. We have been offered a unique opportunity.

Pierre Pagé has taken courses in group psychology, and what he has learned may come in handy in helping him deal with this case.

So often, coaches who work in professional sports are criticized for being loudmouths who lack perspective and are not very skilled in the art of interpersonal relationships. None of that is true in Pierre Pagé's case. On the contrary, he is reputed to be at his best in one-on-one situations. If only Bonnie agreed to meet with him, or Carl and Eric were willing to listen to what he had to say, perhaps he would open their eyes and help them understand some facts they had no inkling of.

Q. To have effective and productive negotiations, you have to go through three stages.

Q. What are they?

A. The first is "storming". You start off by haggling, then you pour your heart out and finally you yell. Then comes "norming". That's the stage where you get to know yourself better and find out more about the other side as well. The last and most productive stage is "performing". But before you can start being productive you have to go through the first two stages.

Q. Where are you with the Lindroses?

A. We're still stuck in stage 1. That's why it's taking so long!

What also takes time is research, and Pagé, like Bob Johnson with whom he once worked, is always asking questions. He consults with everybody and reads everything he can lay his hands on in hopes of finding new solutions to all sorts of problems related to team sports.

A. We have to keep searching, to study other sports which have had problems similar to ours. They might be able to tell us something.

Actually, the Lindroses do not know what they are missing by not sitting down at the table with Pagé. Their son could benefit greatly from getting to know this upright, honest man who is so devoted to sports.

That is what the Nordiques' strategy, as secretive and obscure as it seemed to be, was really all about — bringing the Lindroses to the negotiating table. If only the two parties agreed to sit down together, there might be some progress. Marcel Aubut stresses that what he wants is for all parties to keep a clear head and sit down and say plainly and honestly what is on their minds. According to him, the few times that the two groups have met, things went well.

A. I have seen the father twice, officially. First in Quebec for a day and a half of meetings. Then in Toronto, with Rick Curran and Gordon Kirke. The two meetings were conducted very professionally.

Q. Marcel, the thing has gotten really big, don't you think?

A. Gigantic! That's why I'm trying not to get too emotional. I have to find a strategy and follow it to the letter. I have one now, and it's progressing, step by step, and stage by stage. We can't change direction every time the wind blows—we have to stay on course. That's the only way we can succeed.

Good luck, Marcel.

Chapter 7

CARL AND BONNIE

At the present time, as a result of a merger between two large firms, one American, the other European, Peat Marwick Thorne is the largest accounting firm in the world. In Toronto alone, the company employs more than a thousand people.

The firm's main source of revenue obviously comes from auditing, but their staff also have other areas of expertise. They often handle bankruptcy settlements and act as business management consultants.

Carl Lindros is a partner with Peat Marwick Thorne; a position that requires a minimum of 8 years of dedicated service, and means devoting much of one's life to the company. Because his area of expertise is high technology, his job is both demanding and risky. In his field, he is the best-known Peat Marwick Thorne employee in Canada. A top consultant such as Carl Lindros can obviously do very well financially, and in good years his income can be as high as $250,000.

Until very recently, it would have been true to say that his work with Peat Marwick Thorne was Carl Lindros's primary interest. However, the emergence of Eric Lindros on the hockey scene has unquestionably led to a shift in Carl's priorities. It is easy to predict that, in the very near future, management of his son's business interests will probably take precedence over everything else.

By coincidence, Jerome Dupont, a former NHL hockey player, was also one of Peat Marwick Thorne's many employees. Jerome played for the Chicago Black Hawks and the Toronto Maple Leafs before hanging up his skates when he was only twenty-six years old. He is one of a small but gradually increasing number of professional athletes who have university degrees. Jerome has already earned one degree, will soon receive his second and hopes to work on a third if things go according to plan.

Also by coincidence, Carl and Jerome had on occasion worked together on the same project, so of course it was inevitable that the conversation would sometimes turn to Eric and his career plans. I talked to Jerome about conversations he had had with Carl.

Q. Did you often have a chance to talk about Eric?

A. Not really, but we did talk about him once in awhile.

Q. And what do you think about the whole situation?

A. First, I'd have to say that it's very emotional. You can tell that it's really bothering him.

Q. Does he talk about it easily?

A. Not usually. I'd say he's very careful.

Q. Did you learn anything anyway?

A. Oh yes. He did come to say something just because we happened to be talking.

It was easy to see that Jerome was also being careful. Even though he was not afraid of the consequences of what he might say, he wanted to be sure that anything he reported was as close to the truth as possible.

A. Eric is in a very difficult situation. Carl is convinced that the Quebec market is not worth half of what the market would be in a large American city like New York or Chicago.

Q. Then he really is sincere in saying the financial issue is the main reason that Eric has refused to go to Quebec?

A. I wouldn't say that it's the most important reason, but it certainly is a very large consideration.

Q. Did he mention the other reasons?

A. Yes. He talked a little about the political situation in Quebec. And it seems to frighten him a lot.

Jerome wanted to get back to the question of money—he is, after all, an accountant. He said that one of Carl Lindros's main concerns is the question of the Nordiques' financial strength.

A. In talking to us, Carl did mention that he had some doubts as to the financial strength of the team and its owners. He does not think the Nordiques will be able to assume the increased financial burden they would have, if Eric's salary were added to the team payroll. With the salary demands of Sakic, Nolan, Sundin and a few others, the Nordiques will not be able to make ends meet if in fact Eric gets the three million or more he would ask for.

Q. Does he talk much about the other Nordiques players?

A. No, except he did mention that Sakic has a clause in his contract that is supposed to guarantee him the highest salary on the team.

Q. Does he have any other financial concerns?

A. Oh yes. He consulted some American marketing experts and they said that income from advertising endorsements in a market like Quebec's would be at least three times lower than in a large American centre.

As for the comparison between Quebec City and Montreal, Jerome confirmed that the Lindroses did think Montreal would not be as bad as Quebec City and that, yes, Eric would agree to play there. But Jerome was quick to add that he was not sure they really meant it.

From my conversation with Dupont, I also learned that Carl Lindros has a good reputation among his co-workers and is generally well respected. Jerome acknowledges that some employees have made negative comments about Carl, but he believes that they may simply be jealous — given the fact that Eric and his family have been so successful.

Bonnie Lindros is another story. I would like to be able to report that people have only good things to say about her, but that would be an outright lie. Even those who try to say something nice about Bonnie feel bound to qualify their statements. One thing is certain in any case: she does not leave anyone indifferent. You also get the impression listening to people talk about her that she is not one to go unnoticed and that she tends to dominate whatever room she is in.

From the time the Lindros family arrived in Toronto, people in their immediate neighbourhood started talking about them. Even then, when he was just a child, people were praising Eric and usually said something like: "What a talented little kid; he'll go far. But his mother—what a pain!"

In that respect, nothing has changed. Bonnie Lindros's involvement in her son's life knows no bounds, as the coaches of every team Eric has ever played for can testify. Even Team Canada coach Dave King has been on the receiving end of Bonnie's abusive comments, and sometimes the advice she hands out so lavishly borders on insolence. Either Eric is not being played often enough or his line mates are not good enough to play with him. Her son is simply the best. Nobody can contradict her and that's all there is to that.

Wendy Jerome is a sports psychologist at Laurentian University in Sudbury. She is full of admiration for the Lindros family, but she can't help wondering about the unusually large role the mother apparently plays in her older son's life.

Q. That's weird. In hockey, it's not the mother who does the talking. I think what we've got here is a marketing ploy.

Q. In what sense?

A. Here we have an attractive woman who likes to have her opinions heard, who likes to be front and centre, and they're using it as sort of a sales pitch.

Q. Everyone who has had to deal with her has found her imposing. She seems to dominate, maybe too much according to those closest to her. Do you think that's good for Eric's development?

A. Some women are very protective of their children and it could be that she's that way. It seems to be working. It's a very tight unit. Eric really admires his mother; he sees her as the doer and the protector.

Wendy uses Eric's autobiography as a basis for her analysis of the Lindroses. She is well aware that only a partial picture emerges from the book, since, in effect, the authors leave out anything that does not present Eric and his family in a positive light. However, she has managed to read between the lines.

A. I've never seen a kid who has this attitude towards practising, who wants to be as good as he can be at something — that kind of a work ethic. Most of the kids will play for fun, but he seems to constantly be working, working, working to correct skills. He seems to be a fairly normal kid except he seems to have an enormous need to perfect what he's doing. He's very goal-oriented, and until he resolves his competitive goal, there's not a lot of room in his life for anything else.

What came out of my conversation with Wendy Jerome was that the Lindroses are a model, exemplary family who would be the envy of most parents whose ambitions for their own children are similar to those of Carl and Bonnie. The catch is that the results are often not up to the level of expectation. In addition, Eric is tremendously dependent on his parents and he will continue to depend on them for a long time because he needs their support, encouragement and approval for every step he takes. Wendy Jerome had this to say:

A. I've worked with a couple of Canadian athletes whose productivity diminished when they had to leave home. I think that Eric Lindros needs this support group still. I would see him having problems if he was left on his own.

We ended our conversation on a positive note, and Wendy seemed to need to add this to her admiration of the Lindros family:

A. It's too good to be true!

You have to admit that the Lindros family deserves the praise it gets from most observers. They are successful in that their children glow with the joy of living, and they are the envy of most of the people around them.

During the months I was doing research to prepare for writing this book, I heard all kinds of unbelievable stories about Bonnie Lindros. Were they true or false? Probably half and half. It is worth remembering, however, that Eric Lindros is not suffering—at least not publicly — from his mother's involvement in his affairs. Quite the contrary, he seems to take pleasure in the controversy she causes. One thing is certain. Bonnie has been relentless in defending her son's cause, and until now, her input seems to have made a positive contribution to the advancement of his career.

There comes a time when parents have to withdraw gradually from involvement in their children's lives. From an outsider's point of view, that time seems to have arrived for Eric Lindros. Will he assert his independence in the near future? We can only hope so. However, on the basis of the experiences described in Eric's autobiography, there is reason to doubt that this will happen.

Carl Lindros has suggested that being involved with hockey is a good way to get a clear picture of the Canadian mosaic. It is odd, that, with his understanding of the diversity of the country, he cannot envisage the Quebec option for his son.

Like many other English-speaking Canadians, the Lindroses suffer from a kind of self-righteousness as a result of which they see things only from their own perspective. There is nothing more disagreeable than to try to come to terms with people who are convinced that they are right, that they are within their rights and that they have truth on their side. Furthermore, it is not easy for them to trust anyone who does not think as they do. Eric is an inevitable offshoot of this mentality.

UPDATE

T wo major events have taken place since I finished writing the original French version of *L'affaire Lindros*. Both were played out on the international scene, and they gave us an opportunity to observe Eric Lindros at his best and at his worst. The Winter Olympics in Albertville, France showed beyond any shadow of a doubt that Eric's presence on a talented team could make it noticeably better, while the World Junior Hockey Tournament in Fussen, Germany exposed the defects that can exist in even the most talented of athletes.

From the beginning of the junior championship series, it was easy to see that the members of the Canadian team had their work cut out for them. In the first game, they beat the Germans by the skin of their teeth, 5 to 4, thanks to Patrick Poulin's goal with only about twenty seconds remaining in the game. In defence of the Canadians, I have to mention that a flu bug had considerably weakened several of the players. Because Eric Lindros was one of those who had been affected by the virus, his performance during the game was rather ordinary. Things were so bad that the day of the game, Trevor Kidd, the excellent goaltender the juniors had borrowed from Team Canada, said he was so sick that he almost fainted.

The next game did not do anything to make the Canadians look any better, even though they won 6 to 4, since their opponents, the Swiss team, were not expected to offer a very strong opposition. Nevertheless, the behaviour exhibited by the Canadians throughout the game was totally out of line. They earned one penalty after another, giving the impression that they were motivated more by frustration than by a desire to do anything right. Furthermore, after the game, several members of the team admitted that there was nothing pretty about the show they had put on. Kimbi Daniels, for example, did not mince words:

''It's a farce. The guys have to realize we can't come over here and try to take the other guys' heads off. And that, I think, is what we were trying to do. Canadians have an image of Europeans that we can slap them around and they're not going to do anything. The way we see Europeans is that we can run them over. We can't do that. We have to play under control and stay out of the penalty box.''

As for Eric Lindros, who we must remember was the captain of the team, he let his frustration get the better of him, as illustrated by the unforgivable act he committed at the end of the game just as the Swiss players left their bench to go and congratulate their goalie. Journalist Alan Adams of the Canadian Press described the incident this way:

Standing in the face-off circle to the right of Canadian goalie Trevor Kidd, Lindros whistled a slapshot into the Swiss bench, hitting one of the Swiss players, who, fortunately, was not injured.

"Lindros was responding to a spear in the back by a Swiss player just as the game ended" was the explanation given to the media by a Canadian hockey official.

Adams's report brought the ire of the Lindroses and coach Rick Cornacchia down upon his head, and at the end of the tournament, Cornacchia let him have it in unequivocal terms in front of witnesses. Needless to say, the Lindros clan is not very fond of Alan Adams, who has now been added to the other names on its blacklist.

Q. Tell me, Alan, did Eric say anything about the incident?

A. Yes, but not to me. He said he was sorry and embarrassed, and that mounting frustration caused him to snap. And I firmly believe that the only reason he apologized is because it was reported. Had it not been reported, he would have had no reason to feel sorry.

Q. Would you say that Eric was not in a good mood from the very beginning?

A. I don't think his head was into it.

After Canada's first two rather unconvincing victories over Germany and Switzerland, the third game against the Swedish team was to be the real test. Canada was leading 2 to 1 with only a few seconds left to go when, as a result of an error on the part of goalie Trevor Kidd, the Swedes managed to tie it up. Kidd had left the net to try to recover the puck, but unfortunately, a Swedish player got there ahead of him, and the puck wound up on the stick of Mikael Renberg who just had to push it into the empty net. According to observers, that tie marked the beginning of the end for the young Canadian team. Alan Adams agreed with that opinion:

A. I really think if they would have beaten Sweden, they would have won the title. The Swedes were the best team there, better than the Soviets.

Q. How did the Canadians react to that setback?

A. They remained confident, but it was obvious they were down a bit. The crowds were not helping things.

Q. How's that?

A. They laughed, they booed, they whistled a lot. Mainly at Eric.

Q. Was it justified?

A. His play was sporadic. They expected to see a superstar and they didn't. They got cheated for their money. Yes, it was justified. Then again, his head was not into it and I think some of it was just giving him a hard time, you know, like: "Big Canadian hockey star, how come you're such an idiot, how come you're doing so bad?" I remember a face-off in the game against Finland. You could hear the Finn player say to Lindros, "Hey, Big Canadian Hockey star, let's go", and Lindros said, "Fuck you". You could hear it loud and clear. He really was under scrutiny — his reputation preceded him.

Q. What was the reaction in the press box?

A. A lot of the European journalists were glad to see him fall flat. They were puzzled. Some of them were pleased to see he didn't do so well because of his attitude.

The game against Finland also ended in a 2-2 tie. After that, the Canadians were mere shadows of themselves and suffered defeat at the hands of the Americans, the Czechs, and the Soviets. It was the first time in ten years the Canadians had been beaten by the Americans in a World Junior Championship and it was particularly hard to take. However, Eric Lindros kept his cool after that game and offered this highly objective analysis of the thrashing they had taken:

"We were outscored, we were outbackchecked and we were outplayed in the neutral zone. We can't expect to put the Canadian flag on our backs and think we're going to win. That's not the way it works."

That series was coach Rick Cornacchia's first experience in international hockey and it must have seemed to him as if it would never end. His team did not come up to expectations and his star player was disappointing.

Q. How was the coach at that time, Alan?

A. When asked how much trouble he thought his team was in, after the loss to the Americans, he shook his head, buried his face in his hands, looked up and glumly replied, "Obviously, we need help now".

A. What was your impression of Cornacchia's performance?

A. He made mistakes the way he handled Lindros. And some of the players realized that, you know, there was more than a coach-player relationship. You have to remember that he was the only player allowed to go home during training camp before the tournament. The team went overseas, while Eric went home to rest. I got the perception from talking to the coaches that there were mistakes made and that the team reacted to the favouritism.

Since it was Eric's third year in a row at the World Junior Championship, it was natural to see him named captain of the team. However, many observers felt that he failed to provide effective leadership in Germany. Asked about this, Alan Adams responded:

A. It would have been an insult not to name him captain.

Q. From your point of view Alan, did he behave like a captain?

A. No. He shot the puck at the Swiss! He tried to punch out three Finns at the end of the game. He wasn't always with the team. His behaviour on the bench, well, a lot of times he was silent.

Lindros, to say the least, was not the dominant force he was expected to be at that World Junior Tournament. Many scouts from the National Hockey League were present throughout the two weeks, and some of them openly questioned the wisdom of having Eric on the team. Eric is at his very best when he has to keep up with others who are as good as or better than he is, and there was no one on the Canadian junior team who could provide that kind of challenge.

The failure of the Canadian contingent at the competition was due to other factors as well. The coaches lacked experience at the international level, and they were unable to mesh the individual players into a real team. That thought was echoed by Bob Nicholson, vice-president of the Canadian Amateur Hockey Association and head of the Canadian delegation at the tournament.

"The talent is there. We have a lot of great players who will be excellent professionals, but as a junior team, they didn't come together."

As Alan Adams wrote at the end of the championship, when things go wrong, you can always blame the coaching staff. That is probably why Rick Cornacchia lost his cool when Alan asked him what lessons he had learned from the experience.

Q. What did he reply?

A. He did not really answer. So I just said that I was sorry if I put him on the spot and then he called me a cocksucker, a fucker, an unethical bastard, an asshole . . .

Q. Any witnesses?

A. Oh, fifty or sixty . . .

Q. Really?

A. He just lost control. I thought his frustration level at the embarrassment of finishing sixth was part of it. He had told us in Kitchener that the hardest part of the job was to deal with us guys. He doesn't really like the media. I'm not a cheerleader. I thought there was favouritism, I tried to find out if there was favouritism, I asked members of the team point blank about it, I pointed out my examples, I talked to different scouts and different general managers to see how they felt about it, I asked them what they had heard. I told them what I had heard, what I had seen and what I perceived as favouritism. It got back to him from a number of sources, some of which are my colleagues, and he just lost it! Had I challenged him then and answered him — I don't usually back away from verbal abuse — he would have hit me. Let's put it this way — it was vicious!

Q. And you never saw him afterward?

A. No. I have no reason to see him. I expect our paths will cross.

Q. Do you expect him to apologize?

A. No, I don't. He made no attempt to apologize. They had meetings, it's been discussed, the C.A.H.A. has said they've made mistakes. They're embarrassed by his behaviour, so I have been told.

Q. What was the reaction of the journalists present?

A. They thought it was quite unprofessional.

Q. But they all chose not to report it?

A. Yeah, because some of these guys have to deal with him every day. I don't know why they didn't, Daniel. I don't want to speculate on their motives. I don't think it's fair of me to do that.

Alan Adams is now a member of a growing group of Lindros clan "rejects". Eric does not talk to him any more, nor does Rick Cornacchia for obvious reasons, and definitely not Bonnie.

Q. Did you talk to her in Germany?

A. I had no reason to talk to her because there is so much animosity between us.

Q. There is?

A. Well, I got the perception there is. I tried to make . . . I let her know that enough is enough, let's end this bullshit, because if you're playing such a big role in his life and I'm covering hockey, our paths are gonna cross and there's no point of us, you know, not talking. But I've been told that there's no point, and that I should go to Carl. After I wrote that story about the Swiss, I was obviously, you know, the bad boy. I was in a no-win situation after I wrote that. I had Cornacchia on me, I had Eric on me, I had Bonnie there . . . I'm on the out—completely.

Q. I think I know how you feel, Alan.

A. And Daniel, do I care? I don't. He's just a hockey player.

Among the Canadian reporters covering the World Junior Tournament was one of the veterans of the CBC Radio Network, Fred Walker. A classy gentleman, well-respected not only by his peers but by athletes as well, Mr. Walker has seldom, throughout his career, had negative comments to make about people on the Canadian sports scene. He was not about to blame Eric alone for the failure of the Canadian entry at the World Junior Championship.

Q. It was not a successful event for Eric or for the team, don't you agree? I mean Eric Lindros was not up to it.

A. I don't think he was. I think he'd love to forget that one.

Q. How do you explain the failure of the team?

A. To be perfectly honest, I think they had a novice coaching staff. When I say novice, I mean they had quality coaches from Canada, but they were people who really didn't know the international game and by the time they found out about it, it was just a little too late. It was an embarrassing sixth place finish they had.

Q. Then, how do you assess Eric's performance?

A. When he played in the Canada Cup, he played with guys who would get the puck to him when he could do something with it, and also whenever he was leaving a drop pass or an unexpected pass, the pros seem to be able to pick up on it. The young kids just could not react or they just were not experienced enough.

Q. And what about the rumours about Eric getting special treatment during that tournament?

A. Some of the stories I heard, like people talking about Eric having his own car and all that sort of stuff, I could not corroborate, except that I was told by Mike Murray (P.R. man) that there were times that Eric was driven from one place to another because he was given special treatment after a game for an injury or for whatever reason. I didn't hear any of the players complain about it.

Alan Adams and Fred Walker were not the only Canadian reporters to be in Germany for that championship. Damien Cox, of the *Toronto Star* and Tim Wharnsby, of the *Toronto Sun* also covered the whole tournament. Tim is a young journalist, extremely enthusiastic and very honest. He has an added advantage in that the Lindros clan, Eric included, trust him. That is not to say that he is anything but objective.

Q. What is your assessment of the team and of Eric at the World Junior Tournament?

A. The team did not have much on-ice chemistry. I don't know how many different line combinations they tried, but nothing seemed to work.

Q. Is it because they had the flu?

A. That added to the problems, but some of the other teams were sick too. I know that the Soviets — or whatever they are called now — they had the flu too. I think the Canadians never really brought out the emotions, because they got behind the eight ball in the first two games with narrow victories over teams like Germany and Switzerland. They almost played scared from that point on. Maybe they were not prepared properly for international play. As far as Eric goes, he will be the first to admit that he did not have his best tournament over there. I don't think that he was psychologically into it, but at the same time he tried to do too much, and his linemates were not used to that level of play, were not ready for it.

Q. What about his attitude?

A. His heart was not into it, and Eric needs to be highly motivated to be successful. He wasn't, not for that tournament. I don't think he was part of the team. I never saw him out with the guys. Obviously he was spending time by himself or with his mother.

It is clear that talent alone is not enough to ensure an outstanding performance. Like everyone else, Eric Lindros needs a favourable environment to be able to play to the level of his potential. In order for him to give his all, the environment has to be stimulating, and he has to feel both mentally and physically committed. The World Junior Hockey Championship in Fussen, Germany did not really inspire him to try to outdo himself, since he had already participated successfully in the same competition the previous two years. His thoughts were elsewhere, and his heart was not in it. Frankly, it would have been better for just about everyone if he had declined the invitation and concentrated on getting ready to do his part on the Olympic team in Albertville. That was an event that would give Eric Lindros the opportunity to shine and to prove once again, as he had in the Canada Cup, that he belonged with the best hockey players in the world.

The Canadian Olympic team is the pet project of Dave King who is without any doubt a master in the art of leading and directing a group of athletes who represent the elite of their sport. You only have to talk to him for a few minutes to sense that this extraordinary coach knows exactly where he is going and how to get there. I spoke to Dave King after the Olympics.

Q. You must have been pleased with Eric's performance.

A. We were. We thought it was a very important tournament for everybody to play a complete type of game offensively and defensively, because the repercussions of one goal can really be quite large. Before the tournament started, we did a lot of work with the players in terms of "team building", that is, to try to understand the need for everybody to pull their weight in every area of the game, whether it be supporting a team-mate who's playing well or not playing well, to be able to cope with the referee, all those types of things. Eric really tried to fit in. He tried to play both ways for us, and we thought it was a very good experience for us and for Eric because the hockey players that did expect him to pick up the puck and go end to end every time he was on the ice, well, at this level it's not possible. At this level you've also got to worry about other aspects of the game and Eric bought into that idea and contributed for us in many ways and we were satisfied.

You cannot help noticing how conscious Dave King is of the "team" concept when he talks about hockey. To him a "team" includes not only players but coaches and managers as well. It is a concept that is not always easy to instill into the minds of young people, and it is often necessary to remind players, sometimes the more talented ones, that hockey is first and foremost a team sport.

A. There's no question a lot of top players will have a tendency to think a lot about themselves but I saw . . . (Eric), when we scored and he didn't score, get right in there and cheer with the guy. It wasn't a situation where he was only happy when he was successful. He bought into a team concept and he enjoyed playing for Canada.

That he enjoyed playing for Team Canada is probably true. What is not so sure is whether Dave King and his colleagues were really thrilled to have him around during the pre-Olympic training period. According to a report that first appeared in *The Toronto Sun* and then in *The Chicago Tribune*, King had considered cutting Lindros from the roster because of the headaches and general distractions involved in just having him around. Dave does not deny the story but states that it was grossly exaggerated.

A. There is no question that when we were in Davos and doing our pre-Olympic training, our final training before the Olympic games, there was a period of time where we were trying to get everybody to buy into playing very much a complete team game. There were a few days when I think Eric was . . . I don't think he was ah . . . trying to be disruptive, but there were a couple of days when you could sense he thought we were training too much. He wondered why we were training so hard, why we had so many meetings, why we had the video sessions. So there was a little period of questioning for a couple of days, Daniel. We sat down and said, ''Eric, this is the way we do things. This is now the very intensive part of our program, it's the very end and this is what we feel we have to do to be successful and everybody else is going to do it; therefore, you have to get that idea as well''.

Q. How did he react to that?

A. Very well. The meeting was one where there was feedback both ways. I guess, in his defense, his season's been long. As he pointed out, ''I had a difficult season. The national junior team was disappointing. Maybe it's my own make-up right now, maybe I'm just stressed too much''. I think we both recognized that he was still not relaxed enough. So we sat down with him and talked about it and said, ''Look, this is what we feel you have to do and you've got to be part of it because you will play that role for us''. After that meeting, we were on our way. We could sense then that, logically, he understood where we were coming from, and I think we understood why he was so impatient with so much preparation. It was the first time I think, Daniel, he was exposed to that type of preparation, so it was a new experience for Eric.

Q. Was he a different guy from day one to the last day with you?

A. I hope one thing has happened for Eric. I'm not saying that coaching is the most important ingredient—talent is. But coaching with the player's cooperation, Daniel, you could facilitate a player arriving at another level. You make it easier for a player with a good attitude to become better and I hope, I think it has occurred, that maybe Eric now understands that coaching has got something to offer. I really appreciate the way he tried to play the way we asked him to play. It showed cooperation, it showed he was going to buy in.

My conversation with Dave King lasted a good half hour and it was very revealing, especially with regard to Eric's attitude towards the coaching staff and his team-mates. King ended with the following remarks, spontaneously, as if he wanted to make sure I would include them in the book:

A. The other thing I'd like to say, Daniel, would be this. You're writing a book about this young fellow. There's been a lot of things said about him being anti-French and all those things, and these comments, I think, are not correct. I think he's a player who enjoys playing with all players. One of his best friends on the team was Joe Juneau, a Quebecker. They got along well. They sat together at meals; they both talked a lot together; they spent time on the bus together; and I felt it was a genuine friendship that was struck. It wasn't anything to do with trying to create an image that he was not anti-French. My experience with Eric was that he was a good team person, he related well to all players and it just so happened by coincidence that one of his better friends on the team became Joe Juneau.

My first question when I reached Joe Juneau at home early one Saturday morning was of course related to what Dave King had said. I had never met or talked to Joe before. He did not know who I was and he was not aware of the book I had written on Eric. So we were both quite matter-of-fact at first, and gradually got to know one another better as the interview progressed. As it happened, Joe went to a school in Ste-Foy, near Quebec City, a high school where I was a teacher some twenty-five years ago. That coincidence served nicely as a way to start the conversation. Then I got to the point fairly quickly.

Q. Is it true that you and Eric were the best of friends in France?

A. Oh yeah. You have no choice when you're on a hockey team that wants to reach the top but to get along with everybody, but I think that me and Eric were—I'm not the only one who says it

— we were the biggest scorers on the team. And I think it was important for us to set an example.

Q. You certainly must have heard of Eric before the Olympics. What were you expecting?

A. You hear about the guy in the papers, in the different media, then you get an idea of what he might be like. But you can't really know what kind of guy he is before meeting him. At the beginning, it was kind of tough. I had to adapt. At the beginning it wasn't easy to have a sincere conversation. It took awhile. I think that was normal.

Q. What impressed you the most about Eric?

A. I think it's, uh, it's just his . . . I don't know how to put it . . . uh, his maturity, you know. Let's say he didn't have any choice either. If he had acted like a kid of eighteen, it wouldn't have worked. He had the chance to be with some of the best players in the NHL in the Canada Cup. That had to have helped him become more mature. Then when you talk to him, he doesn't act like a kid of eighteen.

Q. Some observers claimed that your friendship was fabricated. What do you have to say to that?

A. It doesn't matter. People can say what they want because, they'd obviously say me, I'm Francophone, him, he's Anglophone — they both just had to save face. But that had nothing to do with it.

The tone of the conversation was very warm and friendly. Joe was soft-spoken and he talked frankly and slowly, weighing his words carefully before speaking. His vocabulary was not at all artificial. Without using too much slang, he spoke in very colloquial French. He didn't try to impress me or to seem more educated than he is. However, Joe has completed some very impressive aeronautics courses—in English, though his first language is French! I could not help asking him how he felt about Eric's opinions on Quebec City and the French fact.

Q. Did the two of you ever talk about Quebec City?

A. We didn't really get into it. Sure there were times when I teased him about it . . . and I wasn't the only one. What I remember is that he didn't have anything against the city. It's one of the most beautiful cities in Canada, even if it isn't the biggest. The four seasons are beautiful—in winter, there's lots of snow and it's real peaceful in summer. He said it himself; it's a beautiful city to visit. The fact that he doesn't want to come to Quebec has nothing to do with the fact that people speak French, that the city is too small, that he can't make as much money as somewhere else. I think it's more the Nordiques organization that bothers him . . . at least, that's how it seemed to me . . .

Q. Did you try to get him to change his mind?

A. Not really. At one point he asked me if I'd be interested in playing for the Nordiques. I said it wasn't the same thing for me. After all, I'm from Quebec City, it's my city and I'd be proud to play for the Nordiques. As for Eric, he'd have more pride playing for Toronto than I would for the Maple Leafs.

That was a perfectly natural reflection. In the normal course of events, it makes sense that a player from Quebec would want to be with the Nordiques, while an Ontario youngster dreams of wearing a Maple Leaf uniform. What is striking about Joe Juneau's comments, however, is that he respects the stand taken by his team-mate. It is only logical that Juneau and Lindros managed to become friends to some degree. After all, the two players were representing their country and had a common objective — to do well in front of the cameras of the entire world in the hope of displaying their talents. They both succeeded in playing their game well and each made a contribution to Canada's success in the Olympic games in his own way. Eric Lindros had already been given a great deal of publicity before the games even began. Joe Juneau, on the other hand, was something of a question mark. Neither the general public nor the members of the press knew much about him, but he soon caught everyone's attention and today there is no longer any doubt that he is a talented hockey player.

Brian Williams, CBC anchorman during the Albertville Games, is one man who readily expresses his admiration for Joe Juneau.

A. I think Eric benefited from knowing people like Joe Juneau. I also think that he benefited from playing under Dave King. And I think that whatever team gets Eric will benefit tremendously from what Eric has learned from Dave King. Joe Juneau came away with tremendous respect for Eric Lindros and Eric Lindros came away with tremendous respect for Joe Juneau. I think he learned from Eric and Eric learned from him. And when Joe Juneau speaks of respect for Eric Lindros, I think people should listen.

The fact that Joe Juneau shows admiration for Eric Lindros does not necessarily mean that all is well between French and English Canadian hockey players. It would be ridiculous to conclude that problems do not exist any more just because two men got along over a very short period of time. We have to remember that Eric Lindros still does not want to consider playing hockey in Quebec City, no matter what Joe Juneau means to him. To put things in perspective, let's listen to a man who has been around for awhile. Jim Peplinski, who was formerly with the Calgary Flames, was born and raised in English Canada. Jim is now a colour commentator for "Hockey Night in Canada". He was in France for the Winter Games, as an analyst for the CBC where he had a chance to observe the Canadian team. He also got to know Eric Lindros on a personal basis.

Q. I don't think the Lindroses completely appreciate all the realities, do you?

A. Well, I think that . . . here's another opinion. At times when you're not right up to speed on what's going on in any business, a lot of the time the solutions seem a lot simpler than they are. I think that the solution now for Lindros is very, very complicated. I don't think that there is an easy solution any more. As far as people wanting to know his perspective on the French-English situation, with all due respect and, as I said, I like the guy, I think he's a nice guy, but how can a kid that just turned nineteen have any understanding of something that's been going on for how many hundreds of years? Yet, because he's a great hockey player, people expect him to be perfect in every other way. And I think that's unfair . . . so it does not matter to me whether the guy is a great guy or a jerk, I think what is important is people are expecting a lot more out of him than hockey and I think that's unfair.

An interesting aspect of Eric's personality came to light during the World Junior Hockey Championships and the Olympic Games. Eric showed that he could get very angry, a strategy employed by top athletes when they want to bring their level of performance up a notch. Dave King, for one, considers that ability a useful tool for Eric.

Q. Would you agree that for some athletes, getting mad is better than getting even and that Eric fits that description?

A. I think he does. He's very challenging for himself. He's a classic high achiever. They're never quite satisfied with their own performance, they always think they can do better. There's a time in a game when he'll get angry with himself and he plays better. And I think for a guy who's so intense, so big and so strong, he's very disciplined. I think he only had two or three minor penalties in the whole tournament, and yet he played physically, he played a major role. So really his ability to do that, to play that aggressive game and yet to play it smart, I think that's very important.

Q. I'm also referring to the incident where he kept yelling at Tikhonov, the Russian coach. What do you see in that?

A. That incident along the bench was very interesting. It was a situation where the Soviet defenseman had Eric lined up for a big hit. Eric had the puck. He saw the check coming, passed the puck up and prepared himself for the contact and, essentially, he just ran the player over. It happened to occur right in front of Tikhonov who immediately started to talk to Eric. I don't know what he was saying, it was not in our language, but he was saying something to Eric, and Eric very quickly responded, very, very spontaneously and . . . he's a real competitor. You don't like to see your players get involved with the coaches on other teams, but for Eric, there was no break in his focus. He got angry, he had some words with the coach, he came back to the bench and we said, ''Eric, keep your cool now and settle down''. And he does it right away. The next shift he goes out and it's like nothing happened! He's got the ability to park some of those things and use them to his advantage yet not take it to the point where it's diminishing his endurance. He doesn't get into that situation very often, and that's important for him.

Q. Many players are amazed at what they call his maturity. He was the youngest member of your team. Were you impressed by his behaviour?

A. I think he's mature for his age although, because he's in the spot-light so much, he has to portray himself as being mature — it's a form of survival. What he's gone through with the media and with the public has made him try to establish an image of maturity. Still, he is an eighteen-year-old boy who is really having some fun, while in public he tends to almost protect himself. He becomes very serious, almost guarded at times. But that's what he has to do. He's so much in the public eye, he could not survive otherwise.

Survival could become Eric's new theme. He has already established that he wants to go where he will be happy, and we now have some idea of what it takes to make him happy — a good organization, a group of quality players and a working and cultural environment that meets his goals and aspirations. His next move may well be the most crucial of his career so far.

At the end of the Olympic Games, Eric had this to say:

"There's a million things I've learned from them, the whole coaching staff. Not just on the ice but off the ice, about being a person and accepting certain things."

It would be interesting to know just what those certain things are. We can only hope that his experiences over the last few months will help him make the right choices in the near future.

Although the Quebec option seems to be out of the picture as far as Eric is concerned, Marcel Aubut, clearly speculating on the long-term effects that playing in the Olympics may have had on Eric, had this to say at the beginning of March 1992 right after the Olympic Games:

"I'm still confident we will be successful with Eric Lindros."

When I asked Joe Juneau about the likelihood of Eric's coming to the Nordiques, he quickly replied: "It's totally impossible."

Unless of course, the Nordiques acquired the services of Joe Juneau, Sean Burke, Dave King and . . .

. . . the franchise moved to Hamilton.

Even then, would that be enough for Eric?

EPILOGUE

Cal Botterill is a psychologist who specializes in sports. He knew Eric very well and was with him during the Canada Cup tournament. Botterill acknowledges that Eric is not intimidated by anything.

Q. Do you know that Eric was given some tests?

A. I do know that the National Hockey League did some testing. I have not seen those results myself, but as I watched him during the Canada Cup, I could see that he was amazingly unintimidated and from the very beginning, he appeared to be on a mission. Nothing could stop him. He is so strong, and at times he really was the best player on the ice, without a doubt.

Q. What do you think his reasons are for refusing to go to Quebec?

A. I was amazed at his maturity. He appreciates and understands the adulation he would receive if he came to Quebec. He is aware of how passionate the people are about the game. But he would prefer to avoid it, and that's surprising to most lay people, since most people dream of being heroes or of having that kind of adulation. Yet here's someone who would prefer not to, because of the responsibilities attached. It's an interesting set of reasons that he has — not only cultural or political. The more one finds out about that, the more one understands where he comes from. Here is a man that knows where he is going. Language and culture do not seem to be priorities for Eric Lindros.

Unfortunately, the characteristics referred to by Cal Botterill are part and parcel of Eric Lindros. Lindros may not consider them important, and that is his privilege. However, that is a long way from saying that they can easily be dismissed in formulating a picture of Eric.

Harry Neale, who does the colour commentary for "Hockey Night in Canada", is one of the most knowledgeable observers of this whole story. Both Neale and his counterpart on "La Soirée du Hockey", Gilles Tremblay, are honest, upright and competent — and both are extremely upset by the Lindros case.

I have unlimited admiration for Harry Neale whose style, insight, deadpan humour, intelligence and culture, not to mention his excellent reputation in hockey, make the games he analyzes a pleasure to watch. He even manages to make the Toronto Maple Leafs look good.

I met Neale one Saturday morning at Maple Leaf Gardens and we had a long talk about the Lindros story.

Q. Do you think the whole affair will have a positive ending?

A. I don't really know. I think it's a sad commentary for the National Hockey League and even a sadder one for the country that people who don't live in the province of Quebec have opinions based on nothing in the way of direct experience with living there and yet don't want to do it. NHL teams in Canada are facing enough of a problem with the American-Canadian, north-south split on where players want to play or don't want to play. We are now suffering from a Canadian split, with Lindros in the headlines.

Q. Is he so good he can take such liberties?

A. In many ways he's a very mature boy, quite unlike a lot of the eighteen-year-olds who are drafted, and he does not seem to have the burning desire to play in the National Hockey League any-where, anytime, under any circumstances the way most young Canadian players who get that chance do. And that makes him a little different. I always wonder how a guy like Lindros sorts out the advice he's getting from fifty different directions and comes up with the one that's best for him. Some of his comments have infuriated people from Quebec and rightly so. Most people who get drafted first over-all take it as the biggest compliment of their hockey life. . . . I don't know! It's a tragic story that's hap-pened too often in this country that there is an English viewpoint of Quebec and a Quebec viewpoint of the English part of Canada and I think this is something that gets a little more publicity per-haps, but it's a feeling that's not good for the country no matter what side of the fence you're on . . .

Gilles Tremblay also does not hide the fact that he is unhappy with the Lindroses' attitude towards the Quebec Nordiques.

Q. You must be disappointed by his refusal?

A. Of course I'm disappointed. But what I find even more shocking is that he isn't even giving Quebec a chance to show what they have to offer.

Q. Who do you think is to blame in this affair?

A. The first mistake was giving him so much exposure in the bright lights of the Canada Cup. That gave him a forum and he made good use of it. Then his parents got involved. At this point, far too many people have gotten into the act, and those who should be speaking out aren't doing it.

Q. Who do you mean?

A. The Players' Association first of all, and then the League. Why have these two organizations kept quiet?

Bob Goodenow, the new director of the Players' Association, is aware of the impact Eric's presence will have within the association, and that is probably why he has kept his distance in this matter.

Q. Your association must be optimistic at the idea of Eric becoming a member?

A. There's no doubt everybody will benefit from the presence of an Eric Lindros. The association will benefit by having him as a member because he will make the game better, and as the game gets better it's good for all our members. His presence and skills will create a unique contract for a player of his stature. There's no question that the contract will be looked at and compared by a number of other players. Yes, that will have a positive effect on a number of people.

Q. Your association and the League have kept their distance where this case is concerned. Nevertheless, isn't it true that several people would like to see both organizations take some direct action?

A. It's clearly a case of two parties agreeing to disagree at the present time, and right now I am still hopeful that something can be done to accommodate the best interests of both parties, and I feel that it would not be wise to intervene at this time. The rules are in place as to what the rights are for the Nordiques and for Eric Lindros, and under those rules, both sides are trying to work something out. Then if they fail to do so, there are provisions in place for the next step to be taken.

If the Nordiques and the Lindros clan each hold out as they seem to be doing, you have to wonder where it will all end. The resolve shown by the two sides is bordering on obstinacy. Without the intervention of a third party, it is difficult to imagine a conclusion that would satisfy both these groups. And since the National Hockey League and the Players' Association seem intent on staying out of the matter, there does not really appear to be anyone else who could intervene in the conflict, unless a mediator could be found who was competent, neutral and able to convince the two groups to listen to what he had to say.

I happen to know someone who would be perfect for the job, but he has requested that I not divulge his name for the time being. Suffice it to say that he is highly respected, that his name is as well known in political circles as in the world of hockey, that he has a law degree, that he is bilingual and that he has lived in both Ontario and Quebec. Above all, the Lindroses, whom he does not know personally, could not wish for a better advisor.

I spoke to this exceptional man for almost an hour. Of all the conversations I have had about the Lindros affair, this man offered the most insightful analysis I have heard, touching on every sensitive issue in the dispute.

I am only waiting for a signal from the two clans before I suggest that this man become involved in the case.

* * *

"It is a question of basic intelligence that disposes us to be open to others, having sufficient qualities in common with them to want to ask questions about their differences, find the reasons for these differences and thus reach an understanding of what the differences are."[11]

This reflection comes from Bernard Lonergan, one of this century's most brilliant philosophers and thinkers. Lonergan was born in Quebec, but in his later years he made Regis College in Toronto his spiritual and intellectual home, and he died in Toronto in 1984.

Although Lonergan's philosophy may seem dry at first, it can nevertheless be understood by those who are open-minded and curious enough to want to better understand human nature. Without mean-

---

11 Translated from Lonergan, Bernard, *Pour une méthodologie philosophique*, Bellarmin, 1991.

ing to preach to the Lindroses, I would like to draw their attention to the Lonergan method, which is intended to demonstrate that the various aspects of human nature are all interrelated.

You do not have to be a genius to understand other people. All you need is a little intelligence, just enough to be able to ask yourself what it is that makes them different. Once you discover why the differences exist, it will be fairly easy to learn to understand other people, and ultimately not just to accept but also to appreciate them.

The Lindroses have every reason to distrust the Québécois. It is natural for them, as for the vast majority of Canadians outside of Quebec, to be on their guard with reference to the Quebec situation. After all, to them the Québécois are an unknown quantity, constantly in search of their political independence, which they believe is necessary to safeguard their culture and language.

If only Eric and his family tried to ask real questions, I know they would soon get real answers to the very real problems they are facing.

As Lonergan said, the first step is to accept the differences. They exist and we all know it. In order for two cultures to work together, their people and individuals must accept each other without making any value judgements about the differences they observe. In this way, it becomes superfluous and even ridiculous to try to establish the superiority of one culture over the other.

English and French Canadians have a unique opportunity to live together. The tensions that exist between the two groups are a sign of vitality, and the constant discussions about the division of powers indicate that progress is being made. Meetings between the two cultures may be our best hope for bringing together the two solitudes.

In *Race et Histoire*, Levi-Strauss says that "the single defect that can afflict a group of people and prevent it from fully developing its potential is to be alone".

To be alone also means to isolate oneself. By refusing the Quebec option, the Lindros clan is isolating itself.

The people of Quebec are not seeking to isolate themselves. On the contrary, their desire to assert themselves as a nation is their way of saying that they want to open a window on the world and at the same time open their world to others.

When Eric Lindros says he does not want to take a chance in Quebec, it is because he is uncomfortable with the differences he sees. These feelings stem from the fact that his assessment of the differences is based on a value judgement. But if the two sides hope to cooperate with each other or to derive any benefit from an agreement, they must not judge one another. They must accept each other with all their differences.

All his life, Eric Lindros has been told he was the best. The truth is, he is better than most. However, he has to face the fact that his superiority applies only to the realm of hockey.

When he calls players "frogs", he is confusing the issue, because he seems to believe he is superior to them, not as a hockey player but as an English Canadian.

If Eric were willing to listen to people other than those who are and always have been around him, he would probably begin to see and learn about other realities. And his increased awareness would make him a more complete, more interesting human being.

Three common sayings which express eternal truths could enlighten him in his search for happiness.

1. "Think before you speak."

Daniel Marois, of the Toronto Maple Leafs, doesn't have much to say about the Lindros situation. But he did say this:

"He doesn't think much before he speaks. He is bombarded with questions and he talks too much."

Like other young people of his generation, Eric has a lot to say, but more often than not he has put his foot in his mouth when he has decided to say what he thinks. He himself has said that his mother does not know how to keep quiet, and like her, he often speaks without thinking. From now until this dispute is settled, he would be better off if he made the fewest number of statements possible.

2. "It is never too late to do the right thing."

A friend of Eric's told a Toronto journalist he had heard Eric himself say that, if it were strictly up to him, he would like to play in Quebec City. If that's true, Eric, go for it! You are going to have to cut the umbilical cord and stand on your own two feet one of these days.

3. "Only a fool never changes his mind."

It's no disgrace to change your mind. To tell the truth, it is a healthy sign if we can see our mistakes and admit that we are wrong.

All those who know Eric at all well marvel at his talent, strength of character and forceful personality. Eric Lindros is an impressive figure. With all his assets, it is impossible to imagine him failing in any undertaking.

Nevertheless, it does not appear that success is going to be presented to Eric on a silver platter. For reasons he alone understands, he creates obstacles for himself which he then has to overcome. In the world of sports, people often say that athletes experience tremendous pressure because of their need to win. Although Eric is already under a heavy burden, he has placed additional pressure on himself before he even begins his career in the NHL.

When he says that his priority is to find a place where he can be happy, he is expressing a fundamental human desire. The quest for happiness is what keeps us alive. Strong or weak, great or small, rich or poor, everyone, without exception, wants to be happy. However, some people are born to lead ordinary lives, while others are destined for greatness.

It is a tall order for Eric to fill. Not only does he have to meet the challenge of becoming the next outstanding hockey player in a sport that is always looking for heroes, he also has to face the possibility that he may go down in history as one of the greats of his world, a person who will be looked to as a model or point of reference. In trying to fulfil his potential, he will need to be not merely generous but magnanimous. He will have to surpass himself.

The signals Eric has been sending via his many statements to the press do not indicate that he feels ready to fulfil that role. On the contrary, he seems to be almost completely preoccupied with his own self-interest to the exclusion of any other considerations.

For example, his recurring theme, "I want to be happy. I want to go where Eric Lindros can be happy", shows that he sometimes forgets that the team and the spectators are an essential part of hockey. Never, since the beginning of this dispute, have the Lindroses shown any consideration for the fans—the very ones who are going to make it possible for this unique athlete to attain both his goals—fame and fortune.

At present, Eric Lindros has only one concern—"doing what's right for Eric", but the time has come for him to be aware of those around him. If he wants to be respected, he will have to show respect for those who are going to give him the life he wants. We recognize his talent, but what about his character?

In a column devoted to Magic Johnson, which appeared in *La Presse* on November 11, 1991, Lise Charbonneau wrote this:

"When we are young, we need role models who represent all the good qualities, all the power. They feed our fantasies and add a touch of colour to our rather grey daily lives. We hold conversations with them and they never interrupt us. They offer us a refuge when the adults in our lives fail to understand or show any interest in us."

The role Eric Lindros is being offered presents certain difficulties. He is not being asked merely to play a game but to take on a responsibility. If the thousands of young people who are going to worship him all his life are to derive any benefit from his presence on the hockey scene, Eric will have to make constant progress in his own search for personal fulfilment and happiness. It is only natural that, as he prepares to enter a new and demanding world, he might feel overwhelmed.

Eric Lindros is an unconscious victim of contemporary trends. More and more, the future of humanity is being played out in large urban centres, which act as powerful magnets that attract the greatest possible number of investors from almost all parts of the world. This is especially true in Toronto, where Eric grew up, and therefore he is well aware that that's where the power is—not in Winnipeg, not in

Edmonton, not in Calgary, and certainly not in Quebec City. Eric wants to be part of that power trip. He does not want to run the risk of being left behind by going to live in a small town which he believes has very little to offer him. Eric Lindros is attracted by the power that comes with money. With that kind of power he hopes to prove to himself and others that he is the best.

Eric Lindros is so conscious of his talent that he sees himself as the eighth wonder of the world. All his life he has been told by the people he loves and respects the most that he is an athletic genius. Bonnie even managed to put the idea in his head that he could be as good at baseball as at hockey. Bo Jackson had a close call—Eric Lindros was on his way!

The Lindroses did manage to convince the Toronto Blue Jays to take a look at their fantastic son. And they did.

The Lindros clan tried to keep Eric's tryout with the Blue Jays in Florida a secret, in case he failed in his attempt to impress the Blue Jay brass. They were unsuccessful and the news quickly spread through the pressrooms. In the end, Eric received negative press coverage and was treated as a laughing stock. Not only did he fail to convince observers who saw him at work, Blue Jays management were quick to state that any hopes Eric might have for a baseball career were strictly in his imagination.

Blue Jays manager Cito Gaston, who was on site and watched Eric play, had this reaction when I told him that Bonnie thought her son could improve the team overnight.

A. Did she really say that?

Q. Something like that.

A. Well, tell her she should take over my job. She must know something I don't know.

* * *

On November 25, 1991, Ron Sutherland reported in *The Globe and Mail* that "Anglophone Quebeckers are now increasingly bilingual, and most have adapted to the realities of contemporary Quebec". Later in the article he said, "To preserve the nation, what is needed now is a little understanding and generosity on the part of English Canadians outside Quebec".

That is the big question. Do people really want to understand what is happening in Quebec? English-speaking Canadians outside Quebec should stop imagining that all Quebeckers are dangerous separatists.

The Lindroses have certainly not been listening to the counsel offered by Sutherland, an Anglophone living in Quebec. On the contrary, they are quite content to say that they are afraid of the political climate in the province and that they cannot advise their son to go and live in such a dangerous environment.

Their son clearly has every reason in the world to listen to them and to believe them. After all, they have only his best interests at heart. But when will they open their eyes?

And when will the Toronto press stop blindly praising this young man who is just about to begin a human journey which, like all of life's other experiences, is rich with promise but strewn with pitfalls?

Eric Lindros has forced people to take a good look at some situations they have been taking for granted. When he was asked one day to assess the quality of the Quebec Nordiques as a hockey team, he had this tantalizing answer: "I can't judge them, I never see them on T.V."

In fact, "Hockey Night in Canada" almost never shows the Quebec Nordiques games to the rest of the country. All that counts in the eyes of the producers is the large, profitable southern Ontario market. So what do we see on T.V.? The Maple Leafs, or as even the Toronto press at times have called them, the "Maple Laughs"!

"Hockey Night in Canada" never goes to Quebec City. In fact, its reports sometimes ignore the very existence of the Nordiques. For example, on December 28, 1991, one of the few Saturday nights when the Montreal Canadiens were not playing, the French network of the CBC offered hockey fans a game between the Hartford Whalers and the Quebec Nordiques at Le Colisée. At the same time, "Hockey Night in Canada" was offering a choice of games from Toronto, Edmonton and Calgary. From time to time during the evening,

"Hockey Night in Canada" updated the results of games being played in just about every other NHL city. The T.V. audience watching the Detroit Red Wings play the Toronto Maple Leafs saw most of the goals scored in the Los Angeles Kings–Edmonton Oilers game as well as the one between the Philadelphia Flyers and the Calgary Flames. However, not once did they show an update from Le Colisée de Québec that evening.

Quebec is a negligible quantity in the eyes of the "Hockey Night in Canada" producers. Frankly, Quebec seems to bore the people who do the broadcast. On the same telecast of December 28, when the game was drawing to a close and there was a stoppage in play, viewers were shown a summary of the results of all the games being played that day. All the games except one—of course the one played by the Nordiques. What that means to fans throughout most of Canada is that the Quebec Nordiques are of no interest whatsoever.

I would like to use that incident to make a comment on the role CBC-Radio-Canada television plays in Toronto, or should I say the role it does not play, or to be even more specific, chooses not to play. Toronto is the economic and cultural capital of English Canada. The population in Greater Toronto is constantly increasing and will probably be over five million by the year 2000. Of this number, more than 100,000 Francophones are included in this multicultural society that is unique to the country. And that is a conservative number that does not include Francophiles and others who speak and understand French even though it is not their first language.

As of December 1990, CBLFT, the French language station of the CBC in Toronto, ceased to exist as such. In their infinite wisdom, Gérard Veilleux and Patrick Watson, the two heads of the Crown corporation, decided that it was not worth keeping a French-language T.V. station in the largest city of a country whose real nature CBC-Radio-Canada is supposed to represent. This incredible, unpardonable and indefensible action told Francophones in southern Ontario that they did not exist and that, if they wanted to be informed and knowledgeable, they would have to assimilate. In addition, Francophone hockey fans living in Toronto would almost never have any choice but to watch or listen to hockey games in English. Molstar Communications does not deem it profitable to show Maple Leaf hockey games in French.

Therefore, "La Soirée du Hockey" simply does not exist in Toronto, the only city with a CBC French-language channel where it is not shown. You can imagine how Anglophones in Montreal would react if their CBC television station were closed down and then, as if that weren't enough, they were offered Saturday night hockey in French only. And Anglophones in Montreal also have access to a private national network (CTV), a choice Francophones in Toronto do not have, even if they are cable T.V. subscribers. Francophones in the Toronto area are simply second-class citizens, and that's all there is to that.

Like other English-speaking Canadians of his generation, Eric Lindros may very well wonder what the French fact in Canada is really all about when, in his own home, the largest city in the country, people in high places have decided that Francophones are not even worthy of having their own television station!

With his adolescent logic, Eric Lindros tells anyone who wants to listen that he cannot consider a career in Quebec City because the Nordiques organization does not seem interested in putting a winning hockey team on the ice. Then, in the same breath he adds, "But I would be happy to play for the Toronto Maple Leafs".

The comparison is, of course, ridiculous! Since 1967, the last time they won the Stanley Cup, the Maple Leafs have been the worst hockey team in the entire history of the National Hockey League — a situation that is not likely to change in a hurry.

Eric and the members of the Lindros clan would be well-advised to do some serious soul-searching. First, their lack of sensitivity and insight led them to take positions, early on, that had nothing to do with the central issue, and then their inflexible attitude and refusal to negotiate in good faith made the dispute more complicated. In attempting to understand and deal with their situation, they have been using a rather cut-and-dried approach, whereas a little flexibility and imagination might produce better results.

The main issue in this saga has to do with moral and ethical considerations rather than basic logic. In simple terms, the questions that must be asked are these: Do you grant exceptionally gifted individuals special privileges that place them above the laws which govern the proper functioning of an organization? Does talent alone justify the contravention of established rules?

Any social contract is of value only insofar as the members who belong to the group respect its principles. The National Hockey League is an organization whose members are involved in a specific activity. To join the ranks of the organization, either you have to accept its underlying principles or you have to contest them with a view to changing and improving them. If Eric Lindros wants to join the League — imperfect as it may be — he can follow the established procedure and negotiate with the party who controls his rights to play in the NHL, in this case, the Quebec Nordiques. If he is not happy with the situation, he can also contest the established procedure in order to adapt it to his needs. If that is the case, the Lindros clan has to attack the League and its system head-on. The Quebec Nordiques are only one link in a chain, and it is not their responsibility to keep the chain together. It is the League which must assume that responsibility and it is the League that Eric Lindros must approach to achieve his ends. It does not accomplish anything to take it out on the Nordiques. It is not their role to give in to his threats.

If Eric really believes that his potential, which he considers exceptional, entitles him to preferential treatment, he should make his request to the League authorities. He should stop belittling the Nordiques and treating them as his enemy. Instead, he should approach them and enter into frank and serious discussions where there is room to manoeuvre. Who knows? The two parties may even reach a solution that is satisfactory to both sides. The only way to reach any solution is to negotiate, to make adjustments and sacrifices with a view to restoring a situation that has been compromised by unfortunate statements which have only served to increase the tension in an already strained atmosphere.

To paraphrase John F. Kennedy, in what has become a somewhat hackneyed, rather sentimental expression, I am tempted to say to Eric: Ask not what the league can do for you, ask rather what you can do for hockey.

There is no doubt that the Quebec Nordiques represent an immense challenge for Eric Lindros. If he chooses to take up the challenge, the mere fact of his presence will improve a team that is just waiting for a saviour of his calibre to help it reach unscaled heights. He will also help to improve the image of the sport, which very much needs to develop new allies. Above all, if he decides to undertake this daring journey, he himself will grow as a human being. And he will come out the big winner.

ADDENDA 1

A Pair of Skates
Written by Jordana Greenstein (an old school mate of Eric Lindros)

You could say that I live near one of Canada's biggest superstars. The majority of the time he doesn't live in his house because he travels all over North America. He has only recently become a figure in the media and his popularity is on the rise. His new book is due out in three weeks time. His name is Eric Lindros and his house, which is somewhat of a castle, is directly perpendicular to the end of my street. It's rare to see him in front of his house, but I saw him recently playing hockey with two guys who were smaller than him. But then, most *are* smaller than him. His build is more muscular than any guy my age I know.

I met Eric in grade ten when we were in the same typing class. I remember watching the CFTO news and seeing Eric for the first time on TV. It was then that I realized that he was becoming a real superstar. The next day, I mentioned in class that I had seen him on the news and he asked, "So, was I any good?"

I know he must be a bit on the immodest side, but Lindros has some serious fans to contend with. Being in the limelight, this hockey great needs to take extra precautions whenever he's in the public eye. The other day, I was in the car, driving towards the end of my street. You see, if one keeps on driving straight down our street one will end up somewhere in Eric's livingroom. As soon as he saw the tires rolling in his general direction, he ran back to this house to take cover behind the white stone wall in front of his house.

A few months ago, my brother, braver than the king of the jungle, took his bike for a ride with unautographed Lindros cards ready to be signed and consequently gain the worth of a small fortune. He approached the white house and discovered Eric giving his Jeep a wash, so he asked politely for some autographs. Eric acted quite nonchalant, probably because he didn't want to attract too much attention and because his mother Bonnie, also a six-footer, was standing on patrol. Bonnie suspiciously walked over to this interaction between a thirteen year old neighbourhood boy and eighteen year old neighbourhood superstar and warned, "You are trespassing on my property, if you ever dare come here again or tell any of your little friends where we live, I'll call the police!" My brother, totally in shock, retrieved his cards, two of which had been autographed and rode off on his two-wheeler like there was no tomorrow.

Heart thumping and tears streaming down his face, my brother told us about his painful ordeal. On a positive note, he has salvaged two precious autographed cards.

A couple of months later, my mom passed by Lindros' castle and saw an old hockey stick stamped "LINDROS," lying ready for the garbage truck's consumption. So, my brother is now the proud owner of an original Eric Lindros hockey stick! Who knows, it may be worth a fortune some day.

Last night I had a dream that Eric came into the library where I work. Wishful thinking, really. His mom would probably forbid him.

ADDENDA 2

FROM THE OFFICE OF
OBERT J. PULFORD
SENIOR VICE-PRESIDENT
1900 WEST MADISON ST.
CHICAGO 60612

TELEPHONE
AREA 312-733-5500

September 27, 1991

Mr. Jeremy Roenick
262/D Eggleston Avenue
Elmhurst, Illinois 60126

RE: LETTER OF AGREEMENT BETWEEN
     JEREMY ROENICK AND THE
     CHICAGO BLACKHAWK HOCKEY TEAM, INC.

Dear Jeremy:

In consideration of the sum of $1.00, the execution by you (the Player)
the NHL Standard Player's Contract with the Chicago Blackhawk Hockey Tea
Inc. (the Team) dated September 27, 1991, the mutual provisions and
covenants contained herein, and other good and valuable consideration, t
parties hereto agree as follows:

1. The terms of this letter of agreement (Collateral Agreement) shall
    form part of the NHL Standard Player's Contract referred to above,
    and shall be binding on both parties.

2. The Team agrees that it cannot trade the Player or transfer or
    assign his contract to the Quebec Nordiques until July 1, 1993.

                                    Chicago Blackhawk Hockey Team, Inc.

per: William W. Wirtz, President

Agreed and accepted this 27th day of September, 1991

Jeremy Roenick, Player

         CHICAGO BLACKHAWK HOCKEY TEAM, INC.